As tempting as it may be to gift your pastor's or elder's wife with a flowery coffee mug or another potholder with a proverb, give her something more helpful and lasting. Give her Megan Hill's book *Partners in the Gospel*. Each concise and thoughtful reflection addresses a joy or challenge unique to pastoral ministry, offers a corresponding word of biblical encouragement, and presents an opportunity to personally reflect, pray, and act on the good news of the gospel. Give your pastor's or elder's wife a gift that lasts by giving her one that strengthens and equips her to stand firm in the faith.

—**Lindsey Carlson**, church planter's wife; author, *Growing in Godliness: A Teen Girl's Guide to Maturing in Christ*

I am glad to recommend Megan Hill's *Partners in the Gospel* to any woman whose husband is in ministry. Not only are its contents highly relatable, but its application is both challenging and encouraging. It will remind you of what is true, then help you to apply that truth to your everyday life.

—**Aileen Challies**, elder's wife

Having been both a pastor's daughter and a pastor's wife, Megan Hill has had a close-up view of the ministry role of the wives of pastors and elders. It is from this vantage point that she suggests there is "something else" that makes the role of a ministry wife different. With real-life illustrations, Megan explores the joys and challenges of life in the local church. *Partners in the Gospel* is a user-friendly, fifty-day devotional book designed for the busy ministry wife. Visit the book for a moment, or take time for an extended stay. Either way, you will gain an understanding and refreshing friend in Megan.

—**Anne Harley Duncan**, teaching elder's wife

If you're the wife of a pastor or elder, let me encourage you: read this book. *Partners in the Gospel* is full of wisdom, insight, compassion, and perspective. These daily devotions by Megan Hill will remind you of the truth, offer you sympathy in your struggles, and refresh your heart as you walk alongside your husband in ministry.

—**Melissa Kruger**, pastor's wife; author; director of women's initiatives, The Gospel Coalition

Being a pastor's or elder's wife is an important role that comes with very little explanation of the expectations. This can be helpful at times but also hard. Megan Hill knows the joys and challenges of being a pastor's wife, and she lovingly points us to the Savior as we serve and love our husbands and our churches. Hill serves as a trusted friend as she speaks to the myriad of circumstances that a pastor's wife encounters. This devotional is a gift to pastors' and elders' wives everywhere.

—**Courtney Reissig**, elder's wife; author, *Teach Me to Feel: Worshiping through the Psalms in Every Season of Life*

Megan Hill's devotional is beautifully and clearly written. Deeply rooted in Scripture, Megan explores the themes of heart, home, church, and community, highlighting the joys and challenges in each. She is brutally honest about the life of service that is filled with rejoicing, sacrifice, and, on occasion, disappointment. Particularly helpful is the way she connects reflection and prayer with a call to action at the end of each chapter, always pointing to an expression of love for our Savior and thankfulness for the salvation we have in him. Though written primarily for the wives of pastors and elders, congregants too ought to read this, so that they might know how better to pray for those helpmeets sacrificially laboring alongside their elders and pastors.

—**Catriona Trueman**, teaching elder's wife

PARTNERS
in the
GOSPEL

PARTNERS
in the
GOSPEL

50 MEDITATIONS FOR
PASTORS' AND ELDERS' WIVES

Megan Hill

P U B L I S H I N G
P.O. BOX 817 • PHILLIPSBURG • NEW JERSEY 08865-0817

Library of Congress Cataloging-in-Publication Data

Names: Hill, Megan, author.
Title: Partners in the gospel : 50 meditations for pastors' and elders' wives / Megan Hill.
Description: Phillipsburg, New Jersey : P&R Publishing, [2021] | Includes bibliographical references. | Summary: "Focusing on the joys and challenges of the elder's wife's heart, home, church, and community, these fifty short devotional meditations will encourage and equip wives of church leaders"-- Provided by publisher.
Identifiers: LCCN 2020045442 | ISBN 9781629957401 (hardcover) | ISBN 9781629957418 (epub) | ISBN 9781629957425 (mobi)
Subjects: LCSH: Spouses of clergy--Prayers and devotions. | Wives--Prayers and devotions.
Classification: LCC BV4395 .H55 2021 | DDC 242/.692--dc23
LC record available at https://lccn.loc.gov/2020045442

For Colleen, Deb, Eileen, Emily, Kathy, Kristy, and Sue—
my fellow elders' wives.
You refresh me with your friendship,
encourage me by your example,
and delightfully remind me that no two
elders' wives are exactly alike.

CONTENTS

A Word to the Reader | 11

Introduction | 15

1. I Am the Lord's Servant

 **HEART**

Joys | 21

2. Created to Glorify God
3. Redeemed to Glorify God
4. Given the Spirit's Help
5. United to Christ
6. Connected to God's People
7. Granted the Means of Grace

Challenges | 35

8. When You Feel Too Busy to Pray
9. When God Seems Distant
10. When Public Worship Is Hard
11. When You Are Anxious
12. When You Feel Like a Spiritual Fraud
13. When You Are Snared in Sin

Home

Joys | 51

14. Marriage Is Good
15. Working and Worshiping Together
16. Modeling Christ and His Church
17. Raising Elders' Children with Gospel Hope
18. Home Is a Refuge
19. Home Is a Mission Station

Challenges | 65

20. When Family Life Is Busy
21. When You Live in a Fishbowl
22. When Your Marriage Has Hard Days
23. When the Kids Aren't All Right
24. When Your Husband Is Snared in Sin
25. When You Dread Hospitality

Church

Joys | 81

26. The Church Is Valuable
27. Loving the People God Loves
28. Just the Right People
29. Your Elders Are Watching Out for You
30. The Blessing of Corporate Worship
31. Looking for the Heavenly Jerusalem

Challenges | 95

32. When You Feel Like You Are Doing Everything
33. When You Feel Like You Aren't Doing Enough

34. When You Are Home Alone—Again
35. When You Face Unjust Criticism
36. When Church Members Clash
37. When People Leave the Church

 **Community**

Joys | 111

38. You Will Rejoice
39. You Are a Light
40. God Loves to Save
41. Partners in the Gospel
42. Revive Us, O Lord!
43. The Lord Will Wipe Away Every Tear

Challenges | 125

44. When You Suffer
45. When You Are Weary in the Workplace
46. When You Long for Friends
47. When Your Neighbors Reject You
48. When Your Extended Family Is Unsupportive
49. When You Feel Far from Home

Conclusion | 139

50. I Am with You Always

Acknowledgments | 143
Notes | 145
Bibliography | 149

A WORD TO THE READER

My husband has a card that he carries in his wallet. It was given to him by the administrative office of our church's denomination, and it declares him to be an "ordained minister in good standing." It's marked with the denomination's logo and is signed and dated by the stated clerk of the General Assembly. Every year, they mail him a new one. I'm not sure that he ever has to use it, but for twelve months it nestles there in its slot next to his driver's license and his debit card—official proof of his identity as a pastor.

There is no such card for pastors' and elders' wives. I don't have a laminated piece of cardstock in my purse that quickly identifies my place in the world and the church. I can't take it out on days when I'm feeling insecure or overwhelmed in order to remind myself who I am and what I should be doing. And I can't wave it around to remind other people either.

I have spent sixteen years as a pastor's wife—and nearly twenty-five before that as a pastor's daughter—and yet when people ask me to define what the role of a ministry wife is, I still don't have a quick answer.

Sometimes I joke that my job is to keep the pastor alive. Which is partly true, of course. In order for our local church to be shepherded well, the shepherd needs clean clothes and a nutritious breakfast. Most of the things I do every day are pretty mundane and the types of things that lots of other wives do, too: laundry, vacuuming, grocery shopping, cooking.

Sometimes I tell people, more seriously, that my job is to be a faithful Christian and a good church member. This is true, too. Scottish pastor Robert Murray M'Cheyne reportedly said, "The greatest need of my people is my personal holiness." And just as local churches benefit from having holy pastors and elders, they also benefit from having holy pastors' and elders' wives. When I pray continually, commit to studying God's Word in public and in private, seek to be conformed to the image of Christ, put sin to death in my life, worship wholeheartedly, serve where I can, love God's people, and faithfully participate in the meetings of the church, it is the greatest blessing I can offer my congregation. This too is a responsibility that I share with many other women.

But those two job descriptions don't quite cover that indefinite *something else* that also shapes life in ministry. Yes, I care for my husband. And yes, I seek to follow Christ. So should all godly wives. But, as much as we might like to think otherwise, pastors' and elders' wives also have unique circumstances and unique opportunities. This *something else* can vary according to the particulars of each woman, her family, her cultural context, and her church—but it is, nevertheless, present for everyone in ministry. It influences our relationships, sets our priorities, and dictates our responsibilities. It is the reason we say some things and bite our tongues before saying others. It is the reason we volunteer for some tasks and quietly decline to do others. It is the reason people seek us out for counsel and encouragement and the reason they invite us to their bridal showers and birthday parties. It is the reason we sometimes cry on the way home from church. It is also the reason we keep going back.

This book, then, is about all those things. It's about the nitty-gritty of Saturday nights spent getting spots out of a Sunday best button-down. It's about the blessing of receiving the Word and prayer and the sacraments—God's means of grace for all of his beloved people. And it's about that *something else*: the joys and sorrows and expectations and disappointments that belong particularly to the wives of the shepherds of the church.

If you are the wife of a pastor or elder, this book is for you. For the sake of simplicity, I will use the term *elders' wives* to refer to all women married to men who are gifted for and ordained to spiritual leadership in the church. Elders whose primary work is teaching and preaching and who are often paid by the church for their labors (who are sometimes called *pastors*) do have a unique role in the local church (see 1 Tim. 5:17), but it's beyond the scope of this book to address questions of church polity. The Bible itself uses *elders* to refer to all the church's ordained shepherds—including its pastors—and I will do the same here. Whether the church typically calls your husband *pastor* or *elder*, you are an elder's wife, and, hopefully, you can apply the meditations in these pages to the particulars of your own situation.

Being an elder's wife is a joy—and a challenge. Like many of the callings the Lord may place on someone's life, this one brings us to our knees and gives us opportunity to cling to God's goodness. Whether you are new to being an elder's wife or have been in that role for decades, there are probably days when you need refreshment. This devotional is designed to lead you to the only source of true refreshment: the Word of God. As we focus together on our heart, home, church, and community, we will explore both the joys and the challenges that elders' wives experience in each of those areas. As we do, we will see that God's grace is sufficient for every circumstance. Many of the truths in this book are probably things you already know. But it is always good to be reminded.

You may choose to read this book from cover to cover in fifty days, but it isn't necessary that you do so. If you prefer, you could simply keep it on your shelf or nightstand so it's ready for those days when you need to hear again that the Lord knows your situation—and that he is unfailingly good.

INTRODUCTION

1. I Am the Lord's Servant

"Behold, I am the servant of the Lord;
let it be to me according to your word." (Luke 1:38)

I am an introvert. Being around people, talking to them, and sharing in the complex circumstances of their lives eventually makes me feel depleted. That doesn't mean that I'm shy or grouchy; I find people fascinating and truly value their presence in my life. I also always feel like I need a nap after they leave. It's surprising, then, that God called me not only to be part of his church but to be the wife of an elder. From a human perspective, I'm naturally unsuited to invest in the intense relationships of life in God's household. And yet that is exactly what God asked me to do.

Your calling as an elder's wife may be surprising in a different way. Maybe you are a new believer and are all too conscious of your rudimentary knowledge of the Bible. Maybe you are already overwhelmed by your responsibility to parent multiple highly energetic children. Maybe you are daily weighed down by a chronic illness. Or maybe your husband has been called to shepherd a local church in a cultural context that is radically different from anywhere you have ever lived. Whatever the reason, there are probably days when you don't understand why the Lord chose to place you in ministry. You are not alone.

In today's passage, Mary was called by God to an unexpected ministry. She was a virgin, and yet God called her to be a mother. She was young, and yet God called her to disciple the eternal Son. She was from an obscure town, and yet God called her to parent the Savior of the world. It's no wonder that when the angel first appeared, she was "greatly troubled" (Luke 1:29)—and even after he explained, she couldn't quite reconcile the circumstances of her life with God's declared plan. Mary's question, "How will this be, since I am a virgin?" (v. 34), is not that different from the questions that many of us ask. God's call to ministry doesn't always make immediate sense.

But Mary knew the unchanging truth about God and, ultimately, came to rest in it when her life took a surprising turn. She knew and proclaimed God to be mighty, holy, merciful, strong, just, kind, and loving (see vv. 46–55), and she trusted that this God would do only what was right. She knew she was weak, and so God's strength became even more precious to her. She valued God's glory above her own comfort and placed her hope in his purposes more than in her own plans. And, with the help of the Holy Spirit, Mary's humble, faith-filled response can be our own: "I am the servant of the Lord; let it be to me according to your word" (v. 38).

REFLECT. What things about yourself make you naturally unsuited to be an elder's wife? How do those weaknesses cause you to rely on the help of the Holy Spirit?

PRAY. Bring your insecurities and discomforts to the Lord in prayer. Using the words of Mary's song in Luke 1:46–55, praise God for being trustworthy and good. Confess the ways that you lack faith in his purposes, and ask him to help you to make Mary's response in verse 38 your own.

ACT. This week, your calling as an elder's wife will likely challenge your abilities or conflict with your personality. When that happens—whether you are counseling a belligerent teen or hosting a crowd for Sunday lunch—remind yourself of your ultimate identity, and practice speaking this truth to your own soul: "I am the servant of the Lord."

HEART

JOYS

2. Created to Glorify God

*For you formed my inward parts; you knitted me together
in my mother's womb. I praise you, for I am fearfully
and wonderfully made. Wonderful are your works;
my soul knows it very well. (Ps. 139:13–14)*

One of the joys of being an elder's wife is that I sometimes meet newborn additions to our church just hours after they enter the world. As I accompany my husband to the hospital or birthing center, I get to hold tiny bundles who are still drowsy from birth, their downy hair hidden by a knit cap, their wrinkled fingers tucked under a warm blanket. I marvel over each breath that comes from perfect lips and praise the Lord for his answers to our prayers for this new life. Looking at each miniature earlobe and eyelid, I also wonder what the Lord has planned for his newest covenant child. Will she be spunky or quiet? Will she love soccer or stargazing? Will she get married or remain single? Will she write poetry or design airplane engines? In her lifetime, what will this brand-new image-bearer accomplish for God's glory?

As elders' wives, we can easily forget that our value and our purpose in life are much bigger than the responsibilities we have within the home and church. Today's verses encourage us by reminding us that, long before our husbands took church office, God established his plans for us. The Creator of the world set us before his face and paid attention to us. He formed each of our fingers and toes, gave us our eye color and hair texture, determined our height and weight (see Ps. 139:13–16). He also mapped out every detail of our lives—writing each of our days in his book (see Ps. 139:16) and preparing good works for us to do (see Eph. 2:10). Before we cried that first scratchy, newborn wail, our lives had a purpose: to glorify and enjoy God.

Our mouths were made to praise him (see Ps. 51:15), our ears were made to hear his Word (see Prov. 20:12), our hands were made to serve him (see Eccl. 9:10), our feet were made to carry his gospel tidings (see Rom. 10:15), our minds were made to meditate on his ways (see Rom. 12:2), and our hearts were made to love him (see Ezek. 36:26). As elders' wives, we may have unique opportunities for doing each of these things, but our lives' ultimate goal doesn't depend on the current role we're filling or on the specific list of tasks we have for the day. Our entire lives—from birth to death, and then forever—were planned to bring glory to the God who formed us.

No matter where you go in this world or what roles you may fill, you can say to the Lord, "I praise you, for I am fearfully and wonderfully made" (Ps. 139:14).

Reflect. Imagine not being an elder's wife. What in your life would be different? What would be the same? How is the focus of your life sometimes subtly shaped by the responsibilities you have as an elder's wife?

PRAY. Read Psalm 139, and turn each verse into praise for the God who made you and takes care of you. Ask him to help you to remember that your value and your purpose in life are ultimately found in him—not in any secondary role or calling that he may place on your life.

ACT. As you do today's tasks—particularly those associated with the church—remind yourself that you are doing them for the ultimate goal of God's glory. You are a person made in God's image who is serving others who are made in his image. Hospitality, phone calls, intercessory prayer, mentoring, and folding your husband's laundry all find their highest significance in service to the Lord (see Col. 3:23).

3. Redeemed to Glorify God

*We all once lived in the passions of our flesh, carrying
out the desires of the body and the mind, and were by nature
children of wrath, like the rest of mankind. But God, being rich
in mercy, because of the great love with which he loved us
. . . made us alive together with Christ. (Eph. 2:3–5)*

When new people begin attending our church, we try to invite them to our home for a meal. We learn about one another around the table, and, if our guests are believers, we usually get to hear the stories of how they came to faith in Christ. As a result, our small dining room has been the arena for hearing an astonishing variety of Christian testimonies. One woman came to faith by watching a TV preacher who had otherwise dubious theology, and another under the ministry of a faithful church. A guest came to faith during family worship in her childhood home, and another when a neighborhood friend invited him to youth group. One man came to trust Christ while serving a prison sentence, and another after picking up a used theology book from a roadside stand.

I love hearing these stories; in fact, I am often so fascinated by other people's testimonies that I forget to marvel at my own. Today's verses remind all of us to slow down and savor the amazing grace that called us each out of darkness and into the light of Christ. Whether we were called as toddlers or as teenagers, in a season of shocking rebellion or of outward respectability, from the pews of a church or the halls of academia, God poured out his grace on us, covered our sins with Christ's blood, gave us a new identity, and drew us into relationship with himself.

When we affirm that "we all . . . were by nature children of wrath" (Eph. 2:3), it humbles us. We were once just as wicked—and just as deserving of hell—as anyone else who might walk down the sidewalk or through the doors of the church. And when we acknowledge that God "loved us . . . [and] made us alive" (vv. 4–5), it gives us courage. The same grace that transformed the holiest saints is at work in us. Though we often stumble, we can never be disqualified from God's love.

As elders' wives, we can find it tempting to focus on the ways in which God seems to be working (or not working) in our churches, while forgetting to praise him for the great work he has done in our own hearts. When Jesus's disciples exclaimed about the spiritual battles that they seemed to be winning in the world, the Lord acknowledged the importance of their ministry while also redirecting their focus: "Nevertheless, do not rejoice in this, that the spirits are subject to you, but rejoice that your names are written in heaven" (Luke 10:20). Sometimes our greatest reason for joy is the one we most frequently overlook: our own salvation.

REFLECT. What is the most amazing testimony you have ever heard? Do you think of your own story of coming to faith as being amazing? Why or why not?

PRAY. Thank the Lord for loving you when you were still his enemy. Praise him for his grace and mercy. Express your love for Christ your Savior. Rejoice that your name is written in heaven.

ACT. Ask someone to tell you the story of how they came to faith. Tell them yours in return. When the discouragements (or even the successes) of ministry press in on you today, remember to give thanks for God's saving work in your heart.

4. Given the Spirit's Help

"And I will ask the Father, and he will give you another Helper, to be with you forever, even the Spirit of truth, whom the world cannot receive, because it neither sees him nor knows him. You know him, for he dwells with you and will be in you." (John 14:16–17)

In the church, I am frequently asked for help: "Could you help with the nursery today?" "Could you help get these bulletins printed?" "Could you help me to get in touch with that church visitor?" "Could you help plan this lunch?" And those are just the straightforward needs. People's requests for counsel, encouragement, or prayer are often expressed in less direct language, though their desire for help is still obvious.

I'm generally glad to be asked. It's a sign that people trust me to carry their burdens—whether literally or figuratively. But as I assist others with organizing a women's event or navigating their complex family dynamics, I'm also aware of my own limitations. I'm happy to help, but I'm not always very good at it. My failings and inadequacies seem to multiply as I stumble my way through exhortation and encouragement. My thoughts come out of my mouth half-formed, and my tongue trips over gospel truth. Typically, while I'm helping someone else, my own heart is crying, "Help *me*, Lord!"

Thankfully, today's verses remind us that long before we uttered that desperate heart-cry, Christ knew that we would need help. The head of the church knew that the servants of the church would require wisdom, perseverance, holiness, courage, and comfort. He also knew that they would be prone to forgetfulness and fear (see John 14:26–27). So he asked the Father to send help. And he didn't ask him to give just any kind of help; he asked him to send his own Spirit to dwell within us. Although Christ would soon ascend to heaven, he promised his disciples that they would never be alone as they worked and worshiped in his kingdom.

If you belong to Christ, the promised Holy Spirit dwells in you. He is your comforter and your helper, and he will "be with you forever" (John 14:16). What's more, he is the "Spirit of truth" (v. 16) who especially loves to help us to understand and remember the Word of God (see v. 26).

The indwelling helper also enables us to be helpers. When we interact with other believers, the Spirit empowers his Word (see 1 Thess. 1:5), convicts us of sin (see John 16:8), grants us new life (see John 3:6), promotes our holiness (see Rom. 8:4), gives us words to say (see Matt. 10:19), assists us as we pray (see Rom. 8:26), and produces his fruit in our lives (see Gal. 5:22–23). Because the Spirit lives in us, we do not need to "fall back into fear" (Rom. 8:15). Whether we are helping our husbands or assisting another member of the church, we can be confident that the Spirit is at work in us and through us.

REFLECT. What kinds of needs do people in your church or community often ask you for help with? What tasks do you naturally find easy? Which ones most often cause you to cry out for God's help?

PRAY. Read Romans 8:26–27. As you pray for people and situations within your church today, take courage. Although you may not "know what to pray for as [you] ought," the Spirit will help you and pray alongside you.

ACT. The next time someone asks you for help, don't hesitate to cry out for the Spirit's help in turn. Remember that Christ has already asked for this help on your behalf—and what the Son asks, the Father always grants.

5. United to Christ

And because of him you are in Christ Jesus, who
became to us wisdom from God, righteousness and
sanctification and redemption. (1 Cor. 1:30)

In the church where my husband was first ordained, the wife of a previous pastor was a well-known singer and songwriter. Long before I arrived at the church as a newlywed, I had been enjoying this woman's songs—singing them as I went about my days in my adequate (but hardly concert-worthy) soprano voice. Little did I think I would one day be following her as a pastor's wife. Seemingly every home in our new congregation had several of her albums in heavy rotation, and the people spoke admiringly about her gifts. On Wednesday nights, when I tentatively pitched the hymns at our midweek meeting, I was painfully aware that she probably would have picked a better starting note.

Being an elder's wife sometimes means facing unexpected insecurities. Whether you are reflecting on your musical abilities or your teaching gifts, your technological savvy or your theological knowledge, it can be easy for you to think that you don't measure up as an elder's wife.

First Corinthians 1 agrees with you. In that chapter, Paul affirms that most Christians aren't noteworthy. We are neither wise nor powerful nor important, according the world's standards (see v. 26). Rather, we are "foolish," "weak," and "low and despised" (vv. 27–28). We are all unqualified. And it's good for us to be humbled by this piercingly accurate description. In ourselves, we have nothing to contribute to the work of the church, the flourishing of our families, or our own salvation. We can't seem to pitch the right note at prayer meeting, and there are hundreds of other things that we can't do either. Thus, there should be no room for pride in our hearts—we are "things that are not" (v. 28).

Thankfully, today's verse doesn't leave us there. After acknowledging how much we lack on our own, Paul encourages us to recognize how much we gain in Christ. By his life of perfect obedience, his death on the cross, and his resurrection and ascension, Christ redeemed us—and, by his Spirit, he unites us to himself. Throughout the New Testament, the Bible refers to the diverse members of the churches as those who are "in Christ" (see, for example, 1 Cor. 1:2; Gal. 1:22; Eph. 1:1). Ultimately, Christians are not defined by what we can or can't do; we are defined by our relationship to Christ.

And when Christ makes us his own, weak and despised as we are, he gives us everything we could ever need: "wisdom . . . righteousness and sanctification and redemption" (v. 30). His mind dwells in us (see 1 Cor. 2:16), his righteousness clothes us (see Isa. 61:10), his life gives us newness of life (see Rom. 6:4; Col. 3:3), his inheritance becomes our own (see 1 Pet. 1:3–4). And we are joined so closely to Christ that nothing in heaven or earth can ever separate us from his love (see Rom. 8:35, 38–39).

Dear elder's wife, your identity is secure: you are in Christ.

REFLECT. What is something in your life that regularly humbles you? How has your weakness sometimes been an occasion for you to despair? How has it been an opportunity for you to draw closer to Christ?

PRAY. Read 1 Corinthians 1:26–31. Acknowledge your low condition. Ask the Lord to use this to humble your heart. Thank him for uniting you to Christ. Rejoice that in Christ you have everything you could ever need.

Act. When you are tempted to despair over your failures this week, remind yourself that you are "in Christ." And when you are tempted to be proud of some accomplishment, remind yourself that your only ground for boasting is "in the Lord" (1 Cor. 1:31).

6. Connected to God's People

But Ruth said, "Do not urge me to leave you or to return from following you. For where you go I will go, and where you lodge I will lodge. Your people shall be my people, and your God my God. Where you die I will die, and there will I be buried." (Ruth 1:16–17)

Jim came to our church from prison. Raised in a non-Christian home, he grew up having never set foot in a gospel-preaching church. As an adult, he made a series of destructive choices and was incarcerated for several years. A prison chaplain preached the gospel to Jim, and the Lord changed his heart. The Sunday after his release, Jim came to church—and he kept coming. On the day he publicly took his membership vows, he looked out at the congregation and said with joy, "I've never had a people before!"

The fact that we as elders' wives have "a people" may not be something that we marvel at anymore. We don't always maintain the bubbly amazement that we experienced as new members. Often, the local church has become such an ordinary part of our lives that we don't pause to consider how wonderful it is. What's more, being part of an elder's family can sometimes make us feel like outsiders looking in at the congregation. Hurts and conflicts over the years may have increased that sense of distance that we feel. But, however we may feel about it, belonging to the church is for our good.

Today's verse is about a woman who found a people among God's people. The declaration Ruth made to her mother-in-law Naomi was also a profession of faith and a humble acknowledgement that aligning herself with Yahweh would change everything in her life. From the moment Israel's God became her God, Ruth committed to willingly submitting to him. She would come and go at his command. She would live where he called her to live. She would die where he called her to die. And she would join herself to the other people who belonged to him.

We can learn from Ruth's determination to make God's people her people. Before she had even set eyes on them, she had already stirred her heart to commit to them. Like the believers in the book of Acts, who trusted Christ and then immediately joined the church (see Acts 2:41, 47), Ruth lived out her relationship with God by pursuing a relationship with his people. And for us, too, being connected to other believers is essential to the life of faith.

Ruth experienced the goodness of the Lord among his people. God took her out of the loneliness of the world and surrounded her with other worshipers. He met her needs and showered her with love. He secured her inheritance. And he caused her to be both joyful and fruitful. In the assembly of his people, God showed Ruth his grace. Will he not do the same for you?

REFLECT. When was the last time you marveled at the fact that you have "a people" in your local church? Why do you sometimes fail to be amazed by the privilege of belonging to God's people?

PRAY. Read Ephesians 1:22–23. Meditate on the joy of being part of the body with Christ as its head. Ask God to allow you to experience the fullness of Christ in your local church.

ACT. Practice expressing your thankfulness and love for the local church. This week, tell at least one person in your congregation that you love them and are thankful to be part of the body alongside them.

7. Granted the Means of Grace

And they devoted themselves to the apostles' teaching and the
fellowship, to the breaking of bread and the prayers. (Acts 2:42)

In my childhood church, one of our elders' wives baked the communion bread. I can imagine her in her kitchen on Saturday nights: mixing and kneading, adding a pinch of flour to too-sticky dough, leaving the loaf to rise while she attended to laundry or dishes, baking it in her dependable pan, and, finally, wrapping it in paper to deliver it to the church. On Sunday mornings, she sat in the congregation, and her elder-husband would offer her this familiar loaf, baked in her own kitchen, for her to receive as God's gift—a sign and seal of the Lord's covenant and his means of grace for her undying soul.

As elders' wives, we are often intimately involved in the practical details of church ministry. We bake communion loaves, plan Bible studies, participate in prayer meetings, host church events, and set up chairs for Sunday worship. Though the tasks vary from woman to woman, each of us contributes something so that other people can receive spiritual nourishment.

In the bustle of "to-dos," today's verse reminds us that the ministry of the church is not just a task we help with—it's a means of grace for the good of our own souls. The congregation that this verse describes included "all who believed" (Acts 2:44): new converts (see Acts 2:41), apostles (see Acts 1:13), members of Jesus's family (see Acts 1:14), and a faithful group of believing women (see Acts 1:14; cf. Matt. 27:55–56). They were "together," and they "had all things in common" (Acts 2:44). No one, from church leaders to brand-new believers, was absent from the assembly. And not only were they present, they were "devoted." Their lives were focused on being with God's people in the place where God had promised to meet them and on doing the things that God had promised to bless. They listened to the preaching of God's Word, they loved God's people, they received the sacraments, and they spoke to God "with one accord" in prayer (Acts 4:24 NKJV). This wasn't something the mature believers did for the sake of the less mature. It wasn't something the adults did for the kids. It wasn't something the leaders did for the "ordinary" church members. It wasn't a program they offered or a project they launched; it was the whole church doing what God called them to do—together.

For elders' wives, the application is clear: Go to church—not only for the sake of other people but for the good of your own soul and the glory of your God. Devote yourself to the means of grace, and experience all the benefits of Christ's redemption. Focus your life on worshiping God in the assembly of his people, and he will meet you there. Dear sister, Christ's call is a call to you: "Come, everyone who thirsts, come to the waters. . . . Incline your ear, and come to me; hear, that your soul may live" (Isa. 55:1, 3).

Reflect. What practical tasks do you do to assist with the church's ministry? In what ways are you sometimes tempted to think of church ministry as something that you assist with rather than something that is for your own soul's good?

Pray. Thank God for the means of grace he has provided: the Word, the sacraments, and prayer. Confess the ways that you have not received these as gifts that have been given from his kind hand. Ask him to help you to treasure his provision.

Act. This Sunday, when you come to worship, seek to put out of your mind all the practical to-dos that are associated with church life and worship. Instead, feast your soul on the good gifts of God.

CHALLENGES

8. When You Feel Too Busy to Pray

*And rising very early in the morning, while it was still
dark, [Jesus] departed and went out to a desolate place,
and there he prayed. And Simon and those who were with
him searched for him, and they found him and said to
him, "Everyone is looking for you." (Mark 1:35–37)*

"Will you help me find my jacket?" "My tablet won't turn on!"
"Someone's at the door." "Could you come take a look at this?"
"Your phone's ringing in here." "Mommy! Where are you? I need
you!" As someone who is inextricably connected to a husband,
four children, and a local church, I sometimes think "Everyone is
looking for you" could be the Bible verse that summarizes my life.

It was certainly a constant aspect of the earthly life of our
Lord, as today's passage makes clear. A few verses into Mark's
narrative of Christ's ministry, we read that Jesus healed a man
who had an unclean spirit and "at once his fame spread everywhere" (Mark 1:28). Immediately, "the whole city was gathered
together at the door" (v. 33) and were bringing "all who were sick
or oppressed by demons" in the hope that Jesus would heal them
(vv. 32). Quite literally, everyone was looking for Jesus. And Jesus,

filled with compassion, helped them. He healed the sick and cast demons from the possessed. Hour after hour, he tenderly attended to countless individuals who had "various diseases" (v. 34).

We might think that Jesus's busyness—busyness in important ministry to people's legitimate needs—would excuse him from neglecting prayer, but it didn't. Leaving the crowds and their concerns, Jesus "went out to a desolate place, and there he prayed." Our Lord did not allow the insistence of the people, or their focus on their own needs, to distract him from seeking the Father. While we so often allow the constant pinging, ringing, and tugging to pull our attention away from God, Jesus shows us a better way. Our deepest need, and the deepest need of those who are looking for us, is not the concern that is right in front of our faces and begging for our immediate attention. Our deepest need is for fellowship with our God.

And so we must pray. Our love for our Lord should compel us to seek his constant fellowship, praying "at all times" and "without ceasing" (Eph. 6:18; 1 Thess. 5:17). As we pray, we acknowledge our weakness and our total dependence on God. We praise him for his holiness and exalt in his sovereignty. We confess our sins and thank him for his forgiveness in Christ. We seek his help—asking him to give us his Holy Spirit—and we freely submit to his gracious will for us. Through prayer, we express our relationship with the God who made us and redeemed us. As J. I. Packer wrote, "People who know their God are before anything else people who pray."

Reflect. When do you notice your ministry demands colliding with your spiritual priorities? Why do temporal concerns sometimes grab our attention away from kingdom concerns?

PRAY. Before everyone starts looking for you today, pray. Use the Lord's Prayer, in Matthew 6:9–13, to structure your petitions—remembering both big kingdom priorities as well as the daily needs of those who look to you for help.

ACT. The very people who demand our attention are people whom we can pray alongside. Today, when someone comes to you looking for help, invite them to seek God with you. Assist them where you can, of course, but also say, "Let's take a moment to pray together right now."

9. When God Seems Distant

My God, my God, why have you forsaken me? Why are you so far from saving me, from the words of my groaning? (Ps. 22:1)

You open your Bible, but its pages appear shrouded in fog. You go to church, but the worship feels lifeless. You pray, but your words seem to rise no further than the ceiling. You sing praise, spend time with God's people, and look at the beautiful world around you, but nothing moves your soul. You love God, but doubts and sins overwhelm you. You want him to be near, but he is far away.

People might expect that elders' wives are in a constant state of close fellowship with the Lord, but we inevitably experience spiritually dry seasons. Today's verse rose from the lips of two different people whom we wouldn't expect to know anything about spiritual desertion either: King David and King Jesus. David was famously the man after God's own heart (see 1 Sam.

13:14), but there were times when he described God as hiding from him and forgetting about him (see Ps. 13:1). Jesus was the sinless Son of God, and yet he knew what it was like to cry out to God and receive no answer (see Ps. 22:2; Mark 15:34). If God feels distant from you today, you are not alone.

Theologian Wilhelmus à Brakel wrote helpfully about those times when the Lord "withdraws His normal operation, infusion of grace, illumination, and comfort." À Brakel says that spiritual desertion actually has a good purpose for believers. In such spiritual valleys, we recognize afresh that we are sinners who deserve God's wrath, and we consider whether particular sins we've committed have led us away from God. The valley also sharpens our desire for the sweetness of God's mercy, which moves us to look eagerly for signs of the Spirit's work and to throw off all distractions as we seek God alone. He is at work even when he seems distant.

When we are in the valley, we can pursue restored fellowship with God in at least three ways. First, we can confess and forsake any sin that has taken root in our lives. Sometimes, like David, we are spiritually parched because we have turned away from God in rebellion (see Ps. 32:3–5). Second, we can continue to put ourselves in the path of grace. Spiritual dryness can have a variety of causes, but it has only one cure: God's grace. Regular use of the Word, the sacraments, and prayer is God's primary means of drawing us close to him. Third, we can live by faith. Thomas Manton called faith "the empty hand of the soul . . . [which] looketh for all from God." When God feels distant and you feel empty, reach for him. Cling to the promise he has made that he will not cast you off forever (see Lam. 3:31–32).

REFLECT. Are you surprised when you face seasons of spiritual dryness? How does being an elder's wife complicate your experiences with feeling forsaken by God?

PRAY. Using the language of Scripture, express your situation honestly to the Lord. Tell him that you feel forsaken (see Ps. 22:1), forgotten (see Ps. 13:1), and cast off (see Ps. 88:14). Confess to him that you feel he seems to be hiding (see Ps. 13:1), silent (see Ps. 83:1), far (see Ps. 10:1), withdrawn (see Song 5:6), closed off (see Ps. 77:9), and angry (see Ps. 88:16). Acknowledge that this is an experience that many of God's people have had. Ask him to send his Spirit to help you to restore your joy in him (see Ps. 51:11–12).

ACT. Don't give up! Ask a mature Christian friend (or your husband) to pray for you and hold you accountable for putting the three practical suggestions in this chapter into practice.

10. When Public Worship Is Hard

Too long have I had my dwelling among those who hate peace.
I am for peace, but when I speak, they are for war! (Ps. 120:6–7)

I was leaving the church restroom one Sunday night when I heard angry voices down a dark hallway. "And I can't believe he preached that sermon!" someone said. "After what he did this week!" The other person agreed.

I froze, unseen, against the wall. It had been a difficult week; the elders had made an unpopular decision together. But until I overheard those hallway rumblings, I hadn't realized how upset some members were. The worst part was that I recognized the voices. The two people complaining bitterly about my husband were people I had known and loved for years. We had shared meals, visited widows, and attended prayer meetings. Every Sunday, we worshiped together. I felt crushed.

For weeks afterward, I went to church with a heavy heart. I sang the hymns, joined my heart to the prayers, and added my "Amen" to the preached Word, but it felt terrible. I kept wondering what else those voices had said before I had opened the door, and I wondered who else might also be murmuring in the back hallways.

Public worship is a means of grace—but it can be hard. Whether we experience struggles because of an interpersonal conflict, a family crisis, or a battle within our own hearts, it's not always pure joy for elders' wives to walk into church on Sunday. Thankfully, Scripture repeatedly affirms the truth that gathering for worship is a privilege—while also acknowledging that doing so might sometimes be difficult.

Psalm 120, which contains today's passage, is one of the psalms of ascent—the songs that God's Old Testament people would sing together as they were going up to Jerusalem for worship. This is the first psalm in that series, and its opening verse is unexpected: "In my distress I called to the Lord" (v. 1). The psalmist sets out to worship in the temple, but the first thing he experiences is distress. He isn't blithe about going to church, because his life is a tangle of conflicts. He wants peace, but his neighbors want war (see v. 7). He clings to truth, but he's drowning in lies (see v. 2). He's getting ready for worship, but he sees people around him acting like pagans (see v. 5).

As is the case with many of the psalms, this one doesn't present us with a neat conclusion. The psalmist was distressed at the beginning of the psalm, and he's still distressed at the end. But we can learn two important things from the psalmist's example—things that will help us when we have difficult worship experiences of our own. First, the psalmist cried out to the Lord (see v. 1). He didn't keep his frustration to himself; he prayerfully told the Lord about it. And, second, he continued walking toward Jerusalem—toward the place of God's presence. There the Lord answered him (v. 1). When we, too, seek the Lord in our distress, by praying to him in private and worshiping him in public, God promises to draw near to us as well (see Ps. 145:18).

REFLECT. Think of a time when it was hard for you to attend public worship. What factors made it so difficult?

PRAY. Using the words of Psalm 120, express your distress to the Lord. Then use Psalm 121 to thank God for his ever-present help.

ACT. Rather than avoiding public worship, remind yourself that God promises to meet with us when we gather in his name (see Matt. 18:20). Public worship may not always be easy, but it is always worth it.

11. When You Are Anxious

God is our refuge and strength, a very present help in
trouble. Therefore we will not fear though the earth gives
way, though the mountains be moved into the heart of
the sea, though its waters roar and foam, though the
mountains tremble at its swelling. (Ps. 46:1–3)

Margaret Baxter, the wife of Puritan pastor Richard Baxter, was
a woman of great courage. Puritans faced the threat of fines and
imprisonment every time they preached, but Margaret always
urged her beloved husband to be bold. She frequently selected
locations where she felt people most needed to hear the gospel
and arranged for Richard to preach in those pulpits—regardless
of the danger to their family. Surprisingly, however, this same
woman who scoffed at prison and bankruptcy was afraid of illness. She lived with the recurring anxiety that she would lose her
mind, she declined most foods for fear of getting sick, and she
refused to be dissuaded from her conviction that a pain in her
breast was terminal cancer.

I suspect that many elders' wives can relate to Margaret Baxter. We can be zealous and bold in some areas of our lives—
dedicated to the cause of Christ, no matter the cost—while
suffering anxiety in others. We may be happy to move overseas
but worried about leading Bible study. We may be fearless in the
face of church conflicts but panicked over finances. We may be
dedicated to educating our children but hesitant about mentoring a younger woman. Like Margaret, we may face unexpected
temptations to worry.

In today's verses from Psalm 46, the psalmist describes an
alarming series of scenarios: the ground buckles underfoot,
mountains slide into the ocean, and waves whip into a frenzy.
Things that are supposed to be solid give way, things that are

supposed to be high sink low, and things that are supposed to be regular explode in chaos. This is a vivid picture of what we feel when anxiety looms. In those moments, it can seem as if everything is turning upside down.

Thankfully, the psalmist also provides encouragement. In the midst of turmoil and transition, God is an unshakeable refuge for the anxious. No matter how powerful our fears are, God is greater still. He dwells in our midst (see v. 5), gives us help (see v. 5), speaks with authority and power (see v. 6), protects us from attack (see v. 7), and disarms our enemies (see v. 9). All of his plans for us and for this world will certainly come to pass, and he will be "exalted in the earth" (v. 10).

Because of this, we do not need to be afraid (see v. 2). In contrast to the shaking and quaking of our circumstances, we can "be still" because the Lord is God (v. 10). With each wave of anxiety we experience, we can remind ourselves that God is good and he is sovereign. We can cast all our anxieties on him, because he cares for us (see 1 Peter 5:7).

REFLECT. Can you relate to Margaret Baxter? In what situations are you typically bold? In what situations are you prone to anxiety?

PRAY. Using the verses of Psalm 46, confess your anxiety to the Lord. Ask him to remind you that he is in control. Ask him to help you to be still before him.

ACT. Tell someone—your husband, a friend, or another elder's wife—when you are feeling anxious. (If your anxiety is debilitating, also consider consulting a medical professional.) Ask your friend to pray for you and to regularly remind you of God's sovereign care.

12. When You Feel Like a Spiritual Fraud

Jesus said to Simon Peter, "Simon, son of John, do you love me more than these?" He said to him, "Yes, Lord; you know that I love you." He said to him, "Feed my lambs." (John 21:15)

Peter's zeal is familiar to most of us. The first disciple whom Jesus called, Peter instantly left nets and boats in order to catch men instead (see Luke 5:1–11). It was Peter who asked Jesus to invite him to walk on water (see Matt. 14:28); Peter who planned to host Moses, Elijah, and the transfigured Christ (see Matt. 17:4); Peter who protested Christ's crucifixion (see Matt. 16:22) and then resorted to violence at his arrest (see John 18:10). It was Peter who boldly declared, "I will never fall away" (Matt. 26:33).

Peter's assertions of love for Christ were loud and public. His denial was quieter—a brief word here and there in a dark courtyard (see Matt. 26:69–74)—but it immediately produced heart-wrenching grief (see v. 75). As dawn broke on Good Friday, he confronted the fact that his spiritual devotion was not what he wanted it to be.

Peter's bitter tears are the tears shed by all who have lofty plans to follow Christ fully but who know their actions sometimes tell a different story. They are the tears of the elder's wife who affirms the importance of Christlike hospitality but balks at inviting that family with rambunctious children. They are the tears of the elder's wife who encourages others to pray and read their Bibles daily but who struggles to discipline herself to do the same. They are the tears of the elder's wife who wants to practice bold evangelism but fades into silence in front of her unbelieving coworkers. They are the tears of everyone who feels like a spiritual fraud.

Today's verse, along with the surrounding narrative that describes Peter's restoration, can encourage us in three ways when we feel the weight of our own failure to live up to the faith we profess. First, Christ's tender words remind us that our failures are no surprise to him. Although Jesus was not physically present at the time of Peter's denial, he already knew every detail about it (see John 13:38). And after Peter's fall, Christ still sought him out—not in exasperation but in love. Second, this incident reminds us that our sins arise from a lack of love for Christ and that he is the only one who can restore us. "Do you love me?" is Christ's invitation to a renewed fellowship with him (see John 21:15). When we fall, we can go to the very object of our offense for the forgiveness that we need. Third, Peter's restoration reminds us that Christ still uses the weak within his kingdom. Not only does Christ forgive Peter, he also equips Peter to serve others for God's glory (see John 21:15–17). Have you faltered? Hear the loving welcome of Christ: "Do you love me?"

REFLECT. What are some areas of the Christian life in which you have great intentions but sometimes fail to live up to your own zeal?

PRAY. Using the words of Psalm 51, confess your failures to the Lord. Acknowledge that your sin is chiefly against him (see v. 4) and that you need him to cleanse and restore you (see vv. 1–2,

7–11). Ask God to grant you greater love for him and greater strength to serve him (vv. 13, 15–17).

Act. After having denied Christ three times, Peter then declared his love for him three times. Identify one specific area in which you have faltered, and take a concrete step toward obedience in that area today. For example, invite that difficult family for ice cream, pick up your Bible-reading plan, or ask a coworker to a church event.

13. When You Are Snared in Sin

Therefore, since we are surrounded by so great a cloud of witnesses,
let us also lay aside every weight, and sin which clings so closely,
and let us run with endurance the race that is set before us, looking
to Jesus, the founder and perfecter of our faith. (Heb. 12:1–2)

I have a perennial pile of clutter on one end of my kitchen counter. School permission forms, hairbows, books, grocery store flyers, game pieces, and reminders from the dentist steadily accumulate during the week. Anything that doesn't have an obvious solution or a handy location ends up in the heap. I wish I could use that area of my counter, but I have to work around it. Whenever I have guests, I move everything to a less visible location: the top of my desk or an empty cabinet. But as soon as everyone leaves, the paperwork and puzzle pieces return to their usual spot.

Besetting sin is a little like my unsightly pile. Pride, anger, lust, or envy can crowd our lives and make it difficult for us to pursue our callings. A particular sin can even snare us for a period of time. Sometimes our sin may be invisible to others, but we know it's still there. If we belong to Christ, we hate our sin, and yet day after day it keeps piling up. The writer to the Hebrews acknowledges that our sin "clings so closely" (12:1).

It's surprising, then, that Hebrews encourages us regarding our ongoing battle with sin by reminding us that there are witnesses (see 12:1). We might think of witnesses as a threat, not a blessing. But for the people of God, the "cloud of witnesses"—the saints who have gone before us—are our friends as we fight sin.

These witnesses, many of whom appear in Hebrews 11, testify by their own lives to both the cost of fighting sin and the reward of godliness. Abel refused to worship sinfully. It cost him his life, but God commended him (see 11:4). Noah refused to join his neighbors' wickedness. It cost him years of hardship, but he became an heir of righteousness (see v. 7). Moses refused "to enjoy the fleeting pleasures of sin." It cost him comfort and status, but he received an eternal reward (see vv. 24–26). Whether you find yourself battling pornography or excessive spending or impatience with aging parents, these godly witnesses are your allies. They remind you that you are not alone. Your struggle against sin is the same worthy—and costly—struggle that God's people always fight.

But this cloud of witnesses don't merely testify to themselves. They testify to Christ. The saints always look beyond their own weak efforts to see Jesus, "the founder and perfecter of our faith" (Heb. 12:2). Christ endured hostility from sinners, and resisted sin to the point of shedding his own blood, so that we "may not grow weary or fainthearted" in our own struggle against sin (Heb. 12:3; see also v. 4). Even now, he is at work in us to give us the endurance we need (Phil. 2:13). Look to him.

REFLECT. What is one "sin which clings so closely" to you today?

PRAY. Confess your sin to God. Cry out to him for help with fighting it. Ask him to lift your eyes to Jesus.

ACT. Choose one or two of the witnesses who are mentioned in Hebrews 11. Carefully read their stories in the Old Testament, and notice the ways that those saints fought sin. Allow their examples to encourage you in your own battle.

HOME

JOYS

14. Marriage Is Good

Then the Lord God said, "It is not good that the man should be alone; I will make him a helper fit for him." (Gen. 2:18)

As a pastor's wife, I've probably attended more weddings than most people have. I've been to weddings in churches and weddings in historic properties and weddings in backyards. I've been to weddings of family members and weddings of near strangers. I've been to lavish weddings involving dozens of attendants and hundreds of guests, and I've been to small weddings that were planned quickly. Each wedding I attend brings back happy memories of my own.

Weddings are an opportunity to reflect on the blessing of marriage: to give thanks for God's provision for us and to reaffirm our own vows as we rejoice with a fresh set of newlyweds. Today's verse, and the subsequent account of the world's first wedding (see vv. 22–23), similarly prompts us to take a moment to celebrate. In the bustle of ministry life—the elders' meetings and regular hospitality and hurried conversations about congregational and family needs—we must not forget to delight in the fact that God has been good to us by placing us in marriage.

In this familiar passage of Genesis, we read about the final day of creation. On the sixth day, God creates the first image-bearing human being and places him in the garden. We might think that this would be the end of the week's work. But, after hearing God declare each stage of creation to be "good" (Gen. 1:10, 12, 18, 21, 25), we are in for a surprise. God looks at the sinless man in this sinless world and says, instead, that things are "not good" (Gen. 2:18). Something is missing. The man needs a woman. The created order needs the institution of marriage. And so God creates Eve and gives her to Adam. Only then does he declare his world to be as it should be: "very good" (Gen. 1:31).

Through marriage, God provides companionship, makes spouses holy, multiplies his image-bearers, and shows the world a picture of Christ and his church. The Bible does acknowledge that marriage brings with it a variety of constraints and concerns (see 1 Cor. 7:32–35), and it is true that being married to an elder can multiply the anxieties of a wife. But, from the very beginning, the Lord has said that marriage is fundamentally good.

This should be a reason for profound rejoicing, and Adam serves as a prime example of the deliberate joy over marriage we ought to display. God told Adam that marriage was good, and he immediately believed God. Adam's love song for Eve (see Gen. 2:23) didn't arise out of his experience with marriage—after all, he had only just woken up to his newly created wife—but came from his trust that God had given him exactly what was good for him. So we, too, can delight in our marriages even when our circumstances don't feel particularly celebratory. When schedules are busy, when communication stutters, and when married life simply lacks sparkle, we can trust God's kindness and rejoice.

Reflect. Think about the events of your week. What are some practical ways in which you and your husband did good to each other? How do you see the marriage God gave you as a demonstration of his kindness?

Pray. Thank God for ordaining marriage for your good. Confess your occasional lack of gratitude and joy for it. Ask him to give you and your husband delight in each other (see Prov. 5:18).

Act. Follow Adam's example from Genesis 2:23 and verbally affirm the goodness of marriage. Take a minute today to tell your husband that you are thankful to have a life with him. If you have children in your home, say it at a time and place where they can hear you too.

15. Working and Worshiping Together

Greet Prisca and Aquila, my fellow workers in Christ Jesus, who risked their necks for my life, to whom not only I give thanks but all the churches of the Gentiles give thanks as well. (Rom. 16:3–4)

Whatever we might be tempted to think, Paul, the great apostle and church planter, did not labor alone. He traveled the known world, boldly taking the gospel to both Jews and Gentiles and risking his life and comfort many times—but he was supported by a spiritual army of thousands as he did so. Two of the "fellow workers" who came alongside him were a married couple: Priscilla (or Prisca) and Aquila. Though we don't know whether Aquila held church office, he was certainly a prominent servant of the church, and Priscilla and Aquila's ministry marriage can encourage elders' wives today as we labor alongside our husbands.

The first thing we see about Priscilla and Aquila is that they welcomed opportunities to work together for the sake of the gospel. Although they were recently displaced people themselves (see Acts 18:2–3), they offered hospitality to Paul—hosting him in their home for eighteen months and giving him employment in their small business (see v. 11). When Paul later left Corinth to take the gospel to Ephesus, the two of them joined him in his church-planting journey (see v. 18). In Ephesus, the couple mentored the zealous preacher Apollos as, together, they "took him aside and explained to him the way of God more accurately" (v. 26). Later still, they opened their home to be the meeting place for the local church (see Rom. 16:5).

The next thing we see about Priscilla and Aquila is that their shared gospel mission came at a sacrifice. The couple not only incurred significant costs from hospitality and relocation and offered their time and energy for the cause of discipleship but even willingly "risked their necks for [Paul's] life" (Rom. 16:4). As they clung to Christ and set their hearts on serving him together, Priscilla and Aquila learned to hold loosely to their home, finances, reputation, and comfort—and even to their very lives.

And these sacrifices bore eternal fruit. The hospitality they showed Paul allowed the gospel to take hold in Corinth, which led to the establishment of the Corinthian church (see Acts 18:8). Their mentoring of Apollos enabled him to proclaim the gospel with power in Achaia, which strengthened the believers and refuted the Jews in that region (Acts 18:27–28). And the boldness they displayed on behalf of Paul caused him and "all the churches of the Gentiles" (Rom. 16:4) to overflow in public thanksgiving to God.

Elders and their wives have many opportunities for serving side by side. As we attend public worship, visit widows and new babies, welcome people into our homes, offer counsel, or clean church bathrooms, we can thank the Lord for the work he gives us to do together. We recognize that this work comes at a significant cost to us, but, as Priscilla and Aquila did, we can look with eager expectation for what God will accomplish through us.

REFLECT. What opportunities do you have for serving side by side with your husband? Do you welcome those activities? What cost do they require from you (in terms of your energies, resources, and relationships)?

PRAY. Thank God for the privilege of serving him alongside your husband. Ask him to show you areas in which you and your husband can be more generous with your time and energy for the gospel's sake. Ask him to give you hearts that are set on eternal treasure.

ACT. Plan one act of service for Christ that you can do with your husband this week. Ask the Lord to use it to accomplish his purposes.

16. Modeling Christ and His Church

Wives, submit to your own husbands, as to the Lord.
For the husband is the head of the wife even as Christ is
the head of the church, his body, and is himself its Savior.
Now as the church submits to Christ, so also wives should
submit in everything to their husbands. (Eph. 5:22–24)

You probably learned about marriage by watching married people. Your parents almost certainly formed many of your early assumptions about how husbands and wives relate to one another, but you were likely also shaped by the examples of other couples: grandparents, neighbors, friends' parents, church members, celebrities. Perhaps even without realizing it, you witnessed their affection and arguments, their communication and cooperation, their faults and friendship, and you drew from these examples to construct your own ideas about marriage.

The public position you hold as an elder's wife means that many eyes (both young and old) are watching and learning from your marriage. And as they watch, as today's verses make clear, they are learning about more than just marriage.

When a wife submits to her husband and shows respect for his God-appointed leadership, it will attract attention. In a culture that prizes individual autonomy, a wife who seeks to honor and serve her husband is strikingly countercultural. For curious onlookers, this provides a good lesson about marriage—and it provides an even better lesson about how the church relates to Christ. Because Christ is the head of his body and the savior of his people, the church joyfully receives his leadership. Since our marriages follow this pattern, even a quiet moment of cheerful submission to our husbands can become a sign that points friends and neighbors to the privilege that it is to serve Christ.

For the husband's part, when he loves his wife and shows self-sacrificial concern for his beloved's holiness and well-being, it displays a picture of Christ's care for his people. This, too, will be unusual in an every-man-for-himself world and will also point to something that is greater than even marriage. Because Christ's great goal is the perfection of his precious people, he willingly "gave himself up" for the church (Eph. 5:25; see also vv. 26–27). A husband who considers the needs of his wife reflects this same self-giving love.

While it may seem uncomfortable for us to think that every tiff or tenderness in our marriages is a candidate for public scrutiny, it's also an encouragement to our gospel faithfulness. Our marriages were not designed for only us. Our Spirit-enabled successes within marriage—when we treat each other with love, delight in each other's company, and sacrifice ourselves for each other's good—teach the world about Christ and his beloved church. But even when we fail and act selfishly and sinfully, we can testify to the truth of the gospel: God offers abundant forgiveness for those who repent.

REFLECT. What couples have been most influential in the shaping of your ideas about marriage? About Christ and his church? Whom do you notice watching your own marriage and learning from it? What lessons do you think they are taking away?

PRAY. Use Ephesians 5:22–33 to pray for your marriage. While recognizing that every marriage is unique in its particulars, ask God to make your marriage a beautiful picture of Christ and the church—both for your own good and for the good of others.

ACT. Your marriage is important—not simply to you and your husband but also to the watching world around you—and so it is worth your time and energy. Pray about and reflect on the state of your marriage. Give thanks to God for areas in which your relationship is flourishing, and identify an area of weakness that you can work on in the coming weeks.

17. Raising Elders' Children with Gospel Hope

*"For the promise is for you and for your children
and for all who are far off, everyone whom the
Lord our God calls to himself." (Acts 2:39)*

In our church, when parents present their children for baptism, the pastor asks them, "Do you now unreservedly dedicate your child to God, and promise, in humble reliance upon divine grace, that . . . you will strive, by all the means of God's appointment, to bring him up in the nurture and admonition of the Lord?" As we listen to this familiar vow, every parent in the congregation—some of whom are now sitting beside toddlers or teenagers—hears again that God is always the central figure in Christian parenting. Our children belong to him; we raise them only by his grace, we use his means, and we aim for his glory.

We need this regular reminder. Overwhelmed by the daily bustle and struggle of parenting, we can quickly forget that the task of raising children does not ultimately depend on us. It's hard to lift your eyes to the eternal when you are wiping runny noses and shuttling kids between school and sports. What's more, if the people in our churches expect our children to conform to their ideals of what "elders' kids" should be like, we can further lose sight of our kids' greatest need. Today's verse refocuses us by encouraging us that God has gospel purposes for covenant children.

Peter's sermon in Acts 2 is the first recorded sermon following Christ's ascension. Speaking to an ethnically diverse congregation of devout Jews as well as Jewish proselytes (see Acts 2:5, 11), Peter draws the theological line between the Old Testament promises and the gospel promise. He holds up Christ as the ultimate fulfillment of all prophecy—as the Messiah for people in all times and places. And, lest his circumcised Jewish hearers question the position that their children hold in this vast new covenant, Peter affirms, "The promise is for you and for your children and for all who are far off" (v. 39). The gospel will travel more widely than the prophesies that preceded it, Peter says, but it will still have an impact in your homes. God has not forgotten your family. The promise of Christ crucified for sinners is the hope of the world— and the hope of the little one in your arms.

This is good news for parents. The ultimate aim of our parenting is not for our children to be physically safe or healthy. It's not improved performance in school or in sports or on the saxophone. It's not even exemplary behavior—or the approval of church members. The ultimate aim of our parenting is to call our children to trust and obey Christ. We do this by our example. We do this through our discipline. We do this in family worship and at bedside prayer times. We do this by bringing our children under the Word in corporate worship. We do this in faith.

Thankfully, the results of our gospel testimony—like the results of Peter's own sermon—are not in our hands. Instead, we prayerfully look to God and ask him to work in our children's hearts as we raise them for his glory.

REFLECT. What unique opportunities do elders' kids have to hear the gospel? How is life in an elder's family the result of God's kindness to our children?

PRAY. Praise God for the work of Christ. Thank him for blessing you with children. Ask him to help you to proclaim the gospel to them. Plead with him to call your children to himself.

ACT. During family prayer today, let your children hear you pleading with God for their salvation.

18. Home Is a Refuge

In peace I will both lie down and sleep; for you alone,
O Lord, make me dwell in safety. (Ps. 4:8)

In *The Hidden Art of Homemaking*, Edith Schaeffer writes, "There is no specific kind of house you must live in to be 'spiritual'—only the house the Lord has chosen for His chosen purpose for *you*, and the house with you in it." Whether you live on the mission field or in a church-owned manse, in a tiny apartment or a three-thousand-square-foot house, yours is exactly the house that the Lord has chosen for you. It can be tempting to find fault with our homes—we wish they were larger or freshly updated or better suited for hospitality. But our homes, whatever quirks they have, serve God's purposes in our lives and are a sign of his care for us. We can be thankful.

Scripture describes several ways that God ministers to us in the places where we live, and none of them depend on our having a certain type of dwelling. In our homes, we experience God's gift of companionship by enjoying the families he has given us (see Ps. 128:3–4). In our homes, we experience his physical provision by eating the daily bread he supplies (see Acts 2:46–47). In our homes, we experience God's refreshment by freely meditating on and discussing his Word (Deut. 6:6–9). And in our homes, as today's verse reminds us, we experience his peace by resting in the safety he gives us.

For elders' wives, the world and even the church can be places of unrest. As we pursue the cause of Christ, conflicts with sin and with Satan are quick to arise. At the end of the day, we (and our husbands) are often weary. Phone calls, elders' meetings, relationship building, Bible study, acts of service, intercessory prayer, and the constant burden of concern for God's people take a toll—whether it is physical or emotional. And so the Lord, in his kindness, gives us a place to "lie down and sleep." Before an architect ever approached her drawing board, the Lord was designing your home for your good. The Lord, who knows our dust-composed frame, provides us with dwelling places as a refuge. And even if physical sleep eludes us there, we can quiet our hearts before the Lord in the knowledge that he cares for us (see Ps. 46:10; 1 Peter 5:7).

Of course, the four walls and the door that make up each of our earthly dwellings are mere shadows. In the truest sense, God himself is our home. In Psalm 90—the psalm written by the homeless, tent-dwelling, wilderness-wandering prophet Moses—God defines himself as the eternal home for his people throughout all ages (v. 1). He is our refuge from sin and Satan.

He is the source of our comfort and joy. He is our eternal companion. His presence refreshes us. His rules protect us. His Word feeds us. And his sovereign care allows us to sleep in peace—no matter where we lay our heads.

REFLECT. What do you like best about your current home? How do you experience God's kindness there?

PRAY. Thank God for your home. Confess the ways in which you have sometimes grumbled over his provision. Ask him to make your home a refuge from the conflicts you face in the world. Ask him to remind you that he is your true home.

ACT. As you go to sleep tonight, meditate on the ways your Lord has sovereignly cared for you. He formed you in your mother's womb, numbered your days, guarded your steps, and is even now preparing your eternal home with him.

19. Home Is a Mission Station

Give my greetings to the brothers at Laodicea, and to
Nympha and the church in her house. (Col. 4:15)

My parents have a blue guest book in a drawer in their dining room. During the nearly forty years that my dad served as a pastor, the slim volume filled with names. It contains mostly a list of ordinary saints—people whose names are unknown to history. Here and there, a famous name breaks the pattern: an influential theologian, a respected academic, a well-known pastor. But regardless of outward importance, the names in this book represent people who found refreshment in my parents' home before heading out to serve God in their unique callings. Only eternity will reveal what gospel fruit grew from the soil of a good meal, prayer, and spiritual conversation around an oak table.

In the previous meditation, we talked about how our homes are God's provision to refresh us. In this meditation, we will see that our homes are God's provision to refresh others. In fact, our homes are a kind of mission station—a strategic location where gospel efforts can be encouraged and gospel workers can be equipped.

Today's verse underscores the importance of a home used for gospel purposes. At the conclusion of Paul's letter to the Colossians, we read about a woman named Nympha. Her name appears at the end of an impressive list of kingdom servants: Tychicus, the gospel minister (see Col. 4:7); Aristarchus, Mark, and Justus, Paul's fellow-workers (see vv. 10–11); Ephaphras, the great prayer warrior (see vv. 12–13); Luke, the physician and the writer of Scripture (see v. 14); and Nympha, the hostess. Undoubtedly, the men who are in this list did much to advance the cause of Christ in the world. Undoubtedly, Nympha did too.

Although Nympha is mentioned only once in the entire Bible, her house was a hub for kingdom activity. It was the place where the Word of Christ began to "dwell richly" in the assembled Laodicean believers as Paul's epistle was read aloud to them (Col. 3:16; see also 4:16). Nympha's home also provided a place for the Laodiceans to teach and admonish one another, "singing psalms and hymns and spiritual songs" together (Col. 3:16). And, as the assembled church listened to Paul's instructions to Christian families, they may have looked around at Nympha's household for a real-time illustration of those commands (see vv. 18–21). Each of these seemingly ordinary things were vital. In part because of Nympha's hospitality, the Word was "bearing fruit and increasing" among the saints in Laodicea (1:6).

Whether your home hosts women, missionaries, families, small groups, or the entire congregation, it is an important mission station within Christ's kingdom. As you pour coffee or make beds, set out toys or assemble sandwiches, pray before meals or open your Bible for study, you are providing a place for God's people to receive gospel refreshment.

REFLECT. Who have been guests in your home over the years? What different opportunities do you have for practicing hospitality in your current context? How would thinking of your home as a mission station change the way that you view the ordinary tasks of hospitality?

PRAY. Thank God for giving you a home that has a purpose beyond that of meeting your personal needs. Ask him to show you people to whom you could minister in your home. Ask him to bless your efforts at hospitality with eternal gospel fruit.

ACT. Choose an individual or a family to host this week. Consider how you can provide them with bodily and spiritual refreshment in your home so that they will be better equipped for kingdom service when they leave.

CHALLENGES

20. When Family Life Is Busy

*But the Lord answered her, "Martha, Martha, you are
anxious and troubled about many things, but one thing
is necessary. Mary has chosen the good portion, which
will not be taken away from her." (Luke 10:41–42)*

On Sunday nights, after evening worship, my husband and I have
a meeting. Unlike many of our other meetings, this one consists
of just the two of us at our kitchen table. But the whole purpose of
this meeting is to make sure that we don't forget any of our other
meetings. We cross-check our calendars and write in appointments, events, and travel plans. We try to figure out how to pick
up the kids from basketball practice while simultaneously hosting a visiting missionary. We attempt to factor in a week's worth
of traffic and weather in advance. We schedule work and meals,
family worship and prayer meetings—hoping that an extra fif-
teen minutes will appear somewhere. We are never as aware of
the limits of time and space as we are on Sunday nights.

In elders' families, the ordinary obligations of home, work,
school, and church often include additional responsibilities, and
the emotional and mental toll of ministry life can further amplify

our feelings of busyness. It's good for us, then, to turn occasionally to today's passage: the familiar story of Jesus's friends Mary and Martha.

Like many of us, Martha was a woman who felt the pressure of her to-do list. Listen to her as she speaks to Jesus: "Lord, do you not care that my sister has left me to serve alone? Tell her then to help me" (Luke 10:40); "Lord, if you had been here, my brother would not have died" (John 11:21); "Lord, by this time there will be an odor, for he has been dead four days" (John 11:39). Martha wanted things to happen according to schedule, and she worried when they didn't.

Jesus meets her, as her head is in her calendar, and calls her to lift her eyes. "You are anxious and troubled about many things," he notes, "but one thing is necessary." He invites her to lay aside her schedule for a moment and to consider what will be most important in the end: meal preparations or the bread of life? a clean home or a pure heart? physical well-being or eternal life? Jesus invites Martha, the consummate organizer and hostess, to become the guest—to sit at his feet and receive his care for her soul. In the midst of a hundred things to be done, he reminds her to seek the best thing. He reminds her to seek him.

REFLECT. Under what circumstances are you most tempted to be like Martha? What practices help you to cultivate a Mary-like love for Jesus?

PRAY. It's worth noting that Jesus corrects Martha for her misplaced affections and lack of faith, but he doesn't rebuke her boldness. When Martha comes to Jesus honestly, in the midst of her busyness, he befriends her and teaches her about her own heart. If she hadn't spoken up, she might never have grown up. Confess your wrong priorities to the Lord today. Speak boldly and honestly about your frustrations and your struggles with busyness. Ask him to teach you about your heart and to direct your desires toward him.

ACT. As you make your schedule for this week, place the highest priority on fellowship with Christ. Make sure that corporate worship is nonnegotiable in your plans. Mark out time for family worship and private prayer and Bible reading. Trust the Lord that everything else will have to fit around the "one thing [that] is necessary."

21. When You Live in a Fishbowl

Bondservants, obey your earthly masters with fear and trembling, with a sincere heart, as you would Christ, not by the way of eye-service, as people-pleasers, but as bondservants of Christ, doing the will of God from the heart, rendering service with a good will as to the Lord and not to man. (Eph. 6:5–7)

A few years ago, around Valentine's Day, my husband and I decided to go to a movie. We chose a film about a World War II code-breaker, left the kids with a sitter, and headed out. When we returned later that night, the babysitter met us at the door. "My parents texted me that they saw you on TV," she announced, "in line for *that movie*." We were puzzled for a few seconds and then remembered that a violent, pornographic, and highly publicized film was also opening at the theater that night. While we were in line for the dramatized documentary, the local news stations were panning across the crowds who were waiting see the controversial blockbuster.

For weeks afterwards, members of our church met us with grins, winks, and elbows to the ribs. It was good-natured—they knew we weren't actually at the cinema for *that movie*—but the attention they were paying to my private life also left me feeling exposed. Sometimes, ministry life can feel like a fishbowl.

When we are in ministry, many of the choices we make—whether financial, domestic, or relational—will be noted by the people in our church. We are not unlike the bondservants in today's verses, who are always working under the watchful eyes of others. And the Bible speaks the same freeing word to both first-century slaves and twenty-first-century elders' wives: God is your primary audience. Unlike a human audience, God is not capricious or coy. He tells us plainly how to glorify him, and he does not change. And, also unlike a human audience, God is not merely an observer. In the person of Christ, he entered the fishbowl with us. At nearly every moment of his earthly life, Christ was stalked, scrutinized, and scoffed at. He understands our weaknesses, forgives our sins, and sends his Spirit to help us. We may sometimes live under the watchful eye of others, but we always live under the loving eye of Christ.

Through Christ, then, we can extend love to people who watch us. Interestingly, Scripture doesn't rebuke masters for watching their servants or advise servants to keep their curtains closed. In fact, the Bible says that the righteous actions and attitudes of servants are a public testimony of the gospel (see 1 Peter 2:13–25). When we submit willingly, work heartily, and suffer joyfully, we exalt Christ. That fishbowl glass gives us hundreds of daily opportunities to testify to the gospel to anyone who is watching.

REFLECT. In *The Pastor's Wife*, Gloria Furman describes the complexities of "the fishbowl feeling": "There is a safety and assurance that our family experiences in knowing that we are cared for enough by our church body and elders not to be ignored when it comes to keeping watch over our souls. But I think sometimes the fishbowl feeling can take a sinister tone—like your family is the fish in the tank and everyone else is a cat. They're watching you, waiting for an opportunity to strike." When have you felt "safety and assurance" within the fishbowl? When have you felt that "sinister tone"?

PRAY. Read 1 Peter 2:13–25. Ask the Lord to remind you that you and your family are "servants of God" (v. 16) and that Christ entered the fishbowl with you. Then ask him to use your family's fishbowl life for gospel purposes (see vv. 12, 15).

ACT. Memorize Colossians 3:23: "Whatever you do, work heartily, as for the Lord and not for men."

22. When Your Marriage Has Hard Days

Finally, brothers, rejoice. Aim for restoration, comfort
one another, agree with one another, live in peace; and
the God of love and peace will be with you. Greet one
another with a holy kiss. (2 Cor. 13:11–12)

Martin Luther once wryly said, "Marriage is not a thing of nature but a gift of God—the sweetest, the dearest, and the purest life above all celibacy and singleness, when it turns out well, though the very devil if it does not." I suspect that many of us can relate. Even the sweetest of marriages have devilish days—days when both spouses are miserable and when "celibacy and singleness" seem ideal. What's more, as Luther and his wife Katie knew from experience, the troubles of ministry life can strain even good marriages and leave spouses questioning whether this blessed institution is really a gift of God.

Today's verses give believers instructions regarding how they ought to relate to one another—especially when it's difficult. The Corinthian church experienced many of the troubles that also occur within marriages. They quarreled (see 1 Cor. 1:11), fell into "jealousy and strife" (1 Cor. 3:3), acted arrogantly (see 1 Cor. 4:18), led one another to sin (see 1 Cor. 8:10–13), argued about money (see 1 Cor. 9:3–7), behaved selfishly (see 1 Cor. 11:21), failed to communicate clearly with one another (see 1 Cor. 14:13–19), were reluctant to forgive one another (see 2 Cor. 2:6–11), withheld affection from one another (see 2 Cor. 6:12), and even ended up in court (see 1 Cor. 6:5–6). For married couples, this can be a discouragingly familiar list.

It's surprising, then, that Paul's concluding words to these discordant believers are optimistic. "Rejoice," he says. Work toward unity. Look out for one another. Express love. Expect God's help. Paul clearly assumes that relational struggles—even ones that are as bad as the Corinthians were experiencing—can be worked out. Out of obedience to God, we can "bear one another's burdens" and love our nearest neighbors—our husbands—as ourselves (Gal. 6:2; see also Matt. 22:39). The instructions contained in today's verses are simple, other-focused, God-honoring steps that wives can take, with the help of the Spirit, to pursue peace. When challenges arise (and they will!) spouses should persevere in caring for each other. And as we live to please God, we can trust him to work for our good and his glory.

Sometimes, though, even our diligent efforts may not bear obvious fruit. Our marriages may still struggle and face hard days—and weeks and months. But even if we feel distant from our husbands, we can experience God's fellowship. We seek peace with our spouses, and we look for the Lord to give us his peace. We comfort our spouses, and we trust that the Lord will comfort us. We express affection, and we ask the Lord to show us his love. Even if nothing seems to get better in our marriages, we cling to the sure promise that "the God of love and peace will be with you."

REFLECT. What are some areas of your marriage over which you and your husband have rejoiced together? What are some areas in which you need to renew your efforts to care for each other?

PRAY. Use the words of Psalm 27:13 to ask God to show you his kindness during challenging times: "I believe that I shall look upon the goodness of the Lord in the land of the living!"

ACT. Outsiders can help us to strengthen our relationships, just as in these verses Paul strengthened the Corinthians' relationship with one another. If you are having marriage difficulties, you may want to seek wisdom from a mature Christian friend, a pastor or elder, or a Christian counselor. In cases of physical or sexual abuse, contact the appropriate authorities immediately.

23. When the Kids Aren't All Right

Then children were brought to [Jesus] that he might lay his hands on them and pray. The disciples rebuked the people, but Jesus said, "Let the little children come to me and do not hinder them, for to such belongs the kingdom of heaven." And he laid his hands on them and went away. (Matt. 19:13–15)

I know elders' kids—of all ages—who are doing well. Kids who love Christ and obey his Word. Kids who serve the church and seek God's glory. I know other elders' kids—of all ages—who aren't doing well. Kids who can't be bothered to examine their own hearts or to get up for church on a Sunday morning. Kids who resent God's command regarding sexuality or his call for us to suffer. Kids who want to be loved by the world and who want nothing to do with the love of Christ. Simply being an elder's kid is no guarantee of spiritual health—and parents know this all too well.

The parents who brought their children to Jesus similarly had no illusions about their children's well-being. They recognized that their kids had needs beyond their human ability to meet. By faith, they knew that Jesus was their kids' only recourse. The parents in this story were probably not serene and smiling, as they often appear in children's Bibles; like us, the parents in this story were desperate.

And so they overcame every obstacle in order to bring their children to Jesus and plead for his help. They packed up children and supplies; they traveled dusty and dangerous roads; they refused to take the disciples' *no* for an answer. Like the men who clawed a hole in the roof for their paralyzed friend (see Mark 2:1–12), and the mother who willingly compared herself to a dog in order to beg for relief for her demon-possessed daughter (see Matt. 15:21–28), and the woman who elbowed through the crush of people in order to tug at Jesus's robe for healing from her decade-long affliction (see Matt. 9:20–22), these parents wanted Jesus's mercy—and they would not be dissuaded. And as he did for so many others who sincerely sought healing and salvation, Jesus responded to them with love. He welcomed the children, testified to their eternal value, prayed for them, and spoke to their legitimate place in his kingdom.

We bring our children to the same Jesus today. As we urge them to worship, pray for them, speak God's Word to them, and press them to trust him for salvation, we present them to the only Savior of sinners and look for him to work in their hearts. Like the parents in today's passage, we face obstacles as we do this. Our kids' rebellious attitudes, spiritual disinterest, or lethargy regarding the means of grace often make it hard. But Matthew 19 assures us that Jesus loves to hear and answer the prayers of desperate parents.

REFLECT. Can you relate to the parents in today's passage? What obstacles complicate your efforts to bring your children to Jesus? How does having an acute awareness of your children's spiritual need motivate you to overcome such hindrances?

Pray. Thank God for giving you your children (see Ps. 127:3). Confess the need they have for Christ's cleansing blood—no matter how old they are (see Acts 2:38–39). Ask him to call your children to himself and grant them salvation (see Acts 2:39). Thank God that Christ is even now praying for you and with you (see Rom. 8:34).

Act. Your exhortation, your example, and your prayers are important ways to bring your children to Jesus. Resolve that you will make every effort, with the help of the Holy Spirit, to do good to your children's souls this week.

24. When Your Husband Is Snared in Sin

*"If your brother sins against you, go and tell him his
fault, between you and him alone. If he listens to you,
you have gained your brother." (Matt. 18:15)*

Elders' wives are not ignorant of the sins that people can commit. You have likely heard from women in your church whose husbands are snared by pornography, gambling, drunkenness, or filthy language. You probably also know women whose husbands' habitual sins in the areas of anger, dishonesty, laziness, or irresponsibility cause ongoing—if often publicly invisible—pain within their families. Sins entangle even believing husbands. Perhaps they have entangled yours.

Elders are not exempt from sin, and if your husband is snared, the Bible offers you hope. First, God reminds you that he is sovereign over your life—he redeemed you, and he pledges to work out every detail of your life for his glory and your good (see Rom. 8:28). He will use even this hardship to draw you to himself and make you more like Christ. He is also sovereign over your husband's life. The God who began a good work in him promises to finish it (see Phil. 1:6). On the cross, Christ secured victory over sin and Satan—and, although sin is still a fearsome foe, it cannot have final mastery over Christ's redeemed people. Your husband may struggle and fall repeatedly, but, if he belongs to Christ, the Lord will not let him go.

When your husband sins, the Bible also offers you help. God gave elders' wives the resolution and restoration process that we see in Matthew 18 for the good of everyone involved—the good of the sinning believer, the good of the person who has been hurt, and the good of his beloved church. If your husband has been caught in a sin that you cannot overlook (see Prov. 10:12; 19:11; 1 Peter 4:8), then Matthew 18 says that you should "go and tell him his fault, between you and him alone" (v. 15). Speak to your husband—quietly, lovingly, and prayerfully—out of concern for his soul. If he is unwilling to admit his sin and seek the help of the Holy Spirit with pursuing restoration and righteousness, then you should get help. Find "one or two others" (v. 16) who can also confront your husband. Such a helper might be another pastor or elder or a mature Christian friend. If your appeal still has no effect, you and your helpers can approach the assembled elders of the church ("tell it to the church," in the words of verse 17) and let them decide the best course of action.

Ultimately—and regardless of whether it produces any obvious results—it brings glory to God when we respond wisely to our husbands' sin (see vv. 18–19). And that, sister, is our greatest encouragement.

REFLECT. A husband's persistent sin can cause you significant hurt or even drive you to despair. What biblical truths can give you hope when this happens?

PRAY. Although it's tempting to become angry and bitter toward a sinning husband, you will help him best when you have compassion on him and recognize that sin is your common enemy. Elder's wife Janie Street writes, "No matter the magnitude of [your husband's] sin, you must realize the weightiness of your sin before a holy God. Daily recognition of your undeserved cleansing and forgiveness by God will soften your heart toward your husband." Confess your own sin. Give thanks for the forgiveness God has shown you. And ask him to give you compassion for your husband's soul.

ACT. In light of Matthew 18:15–17, evaluate what you have already done to help rescue your husband from his sin. If appropriate, prayerfully move to the next step of the process these verses lay out. If your husband is abusing you or someone else, you will also want to seek help from the appropriate authorities.

25. When You Dread Hospitality

An overseer must be above reproach, the husband of one
wife, sober-minded, self-controlled, respectable, hospitable,
able to teach, not a drunkard, not violent but gentle, not
quarrelsome, not a lover of money. (1 Tim. 3:2–3)

"You can bring her here for supper any time," I said to my husband as we were discussing an elderly church member. I meant it, too. Until the day that he actually did. It had been a rough day—one that was peppered with interruptions and pressing deadlines. The house was a mess, dinner was late, and I was looking forward to an evening's peace. And then the door opened to the unexpected sound of shuffling feet and a creaking walker. My heart tightened with resentment even as I politely welcomed our visitor.

I wish I could say that was the only time I have greeted the opportunity to show hospitality with a sour attitude—but, sadly, that wouldn't be true. Many Saturday evenings have found me nearly in tears over a huge sink filled with dishes in preparation for hosting Sunday lunch. Many weekdays have found me dragging my feet over asking another woman to come over for coffee. Many times I have scrolled through my contacts and known that there are people I should invite over, but I've felt only dread.

If you, too, sometimes lack enthusiasm for showing hospitality, today's verses are an encouragement. One aspect of the "noble task" that 1 Timothy 3:1 says God has given your husband is the obligation to share your home, attention, and resources with God's people. Hospitality is a general command for all God's people (see Rom. 12:13; 1 Peter 4:9)—though these verses highlight its particular importance for elders. This means that God has graciously placed you in a home where hospitality can't be optional. Since he has prepared good works beforehand for us "that we should walk in them" (Eph. 2:10), and since "his commandments are not burdensome" (1 John 5:3), we can trust that God's call to hospitality is good for us.

Today's passage also encourages us with the fact that hospitality is a task for two. Although we may sometimes see hospitality as solely "women's work," Paul didn't see it that way. In these verses, the *elder* is responsible for welcoming people into his life and home. That means that elders' wives are helping their husbands to fulfill their calling—and we can certainly ask them to share the load by making phone calls, going to the grocery store, cooking, changing sheets, or doing dishes.

Ultimately, to be hospitable is to be like Christ. Our Lord prepares a place for us in his Father's house and welcomes us there at exactly the right time (see John 14:2–4). As we repent of our reluctant hospitality and seek the Spirit's help to obey cheerfully, we can have confidence that God is conforming us to the image of his Son—one Sunday lunch at a time.

REFLECT. Why do you sometimes dread hospitality? Think about both your heart attitude and your practical concerns.

PRAY. Read Hebrews 13:2: "Do not neglect to show hospitality to strangers, for thereby some have entertained angels unawares." Ask God to encourage you by showing you that your hospitality has spiritual significance and accomplishes his purposes in the unseen places.

ACT. Consider someone in your church who is lonely or isolated. Invite them into your life and home this week—for a meal, a cup of coffee, or even just a glass of ice water and some conversation on your front porch. Ask the Lord to bless your time together.

CHURCH

JOYS

26. The Church Is Valuable

"Pay careful attention to yourselves and to all the flock, in which the Holy Spirit has made you overseers, to care for the church of God, which he obtained with his own blood." (Acts 20:28)

Most of our churches are outwardly unremarkable. Week after week, the same people show up to do the same things in the same way. To elders' wives, the church may seem especially ordinary. We can recognize everyone's cars in the parking lot and their dirty dishes after the monthly potluck. We know people's favorite hymns and their greatest fears. We can anticipate their needs and deflect their rough edges. Like a well-worn easy chair, the local church is familiar—even comfortable—but it doesn't always seem amazing.

Today's verse, which forms part of Paul's words to the Ephesian elders, reminds us of the church's true value. Our predictable and ordinary congregations are more than they appear. They are, Paul says, "the church of God." In the counsels of eternity, God purposed to love these people, to call them from the world, to rescue them from sin, and to gather them to be his people. In the counsels of eternity, God set his own name on the unremarkable men, women, and children with whom we worship every week. When we belong to the church, we belong to the people who belong to God. Paul then emphasizes the great sacrifice that this church required. It is at Calvary that we see the church's priceless value revealed. The Son of God died so that the church might be gathered and perfected for his glory (see Eph. 5:25–27). Using a remarkable phrase, Paul says that God obtained the church "with his own blood." The church is far from ordinary.

Recognizing this important truth can encourage us—as it doubtless did the Ephesian elders—that every sacrifice we make for the sake of the church is worth it. Throughout his sermon, Paul acknowledges that serving the local church is demanding. He describes his own labors as hard work (see Acts 20:35) filled "with tears and with trials" (v. 19). He says that for three whole years he "did not cease night or day" (v. 31). Then he warns the Ephesian elders that their situation is unlikely to be any easier. He tells them they will encounter wolves and false teachers who will try to destroy the church (see vv. 29–30).

To require these men to pour out their lives for an insignificant human institution or a ragtag social club would be foolishness. But the truth about the church allowed the Ephesian elders, as it allows us, to willingly spend and be spent for the church (see 2 Cor. 12:15). The church has greater value than we can see with physical eyes. It is the beloved, gathered people of God, whom he obtained with his own blood.

REFLECT. As the saying goes, "Familiarity breeds contempt." In what ways does your familiarity with the local church sometimes lead you to devalue it?

PRAY. Confess the ways in which you have not prized the local church. Ask for the Spirit to help you to believe and cling to the truth about the often unremarkable congregation to which you belong. Ask the Lord to help you to serve and sacrifice for the church in light of his own sacrifice.

ACT. What is one thing you have been putting off doing in your church? Perhaps it's a phone call you need to make, a ministry you need to join, or someone you need to invite for dinner. Meditate on the priceless worth of the church and then, in reliance on the Holy Spirit, do that task—in the knowledge that Christ has already sacrificed his very life for the church.

27. Loving the People God Loves

Beloved, let us love one another, for love is from God, and whoever loves has been born of God and knows God. (1 John 4:7)

Although I can count on a few standards, the menu at our church potlucks can be unpredictable. One of our elders' wives will bring her famous meatballs; another member will contribute an enormous pot of soup. And if someone doesn't bring mint brownies, we might all have to go home. The rest of the menu, though, is usually a surprise. While you are standing in line to fill your plate, you don't know exactly what you are going to eat.

The membership of the local church can often feel like a hodgepodge of slow cookers in its fellowship hall. Our congregations come with an assortment of gifts, graces, and personalities. We have college students and mechanics, introverts and extroverts, Bible teachers and people who just want to make the coffee. Some of the members are easy to love. Some of them take a bit more effort.

As is the case with a fellowship lunch, if we come to the church with our own ideas of what we would like to enjoy, we'll probably be frustrated. But if we come to it determined to love what God has assembled, we'll find satisfaction. In today's verse, John reminds us that one of the chief callings of every Christian is to love the people whom God loves. He begins by addressing his readers as "Beloved"—his favorite term for the church. With that word, he reminds us that we are eternally precious to the Lord, that we were bought at the price of his Son, and that we have been welcomed into his family. Then John exhorts us, the beloved ones, to love the other people whom God loves. We haven't chosen them for ourselves, but God has chosen them for himself, and so we ought to love them.

Of course, John knew that loving God's people is rarely easy. He knew this as an apostle and pastor who devoted his life to serving the church, and he also knew it personally. He was the disciple who, at Jesus's command, took responsibility for Mary and cared for her in his own home as if she were his own mother (see John 19:26–27). Because Mary was part of Jesus's family, John loved her at great expense. In the same way, Christ calls each of us to sacrificially love the people whom he calls "my brother and sister and mother" (Matt. 12:50).

Thankfully, we have encouragement as we face this task. "Love is from God," writes John. We do not have to muster up the ability to love God's people (as if we could!). Rather, the Spirit creates this love in our hearts. And, as we receive the Spirit's help, we grow in our own assurance: "whoever loves has been born of God and knows God." When we reach out in love to whomever God has placed in the church, by extending a handshake or a hug, offering prayer or counsel, or giving our time or our money, we rejoice at the fact that God is working in us.

REFLECT. How does God show love for his people? How do you? Consider how well your thoughts, words, and actions regarding the church reflect God's own character.

PRAY. Identify someone in your church whom you have difficulty loving. Praise God that he loves that person—and loves you. Confess your failure to "love your neighbor as yourself" (Matt. 22:39), and thank God for his forgiveness. Ask him to give you love for that person.

ACT. Take a concrete step toward demonstrating love for that person today. Pray for his or her well-being. Send a text or a card. Speak well of that person to someone else.

28. Just the Right People

But as it is, God arranged the members in the body,
each one of them, as he chose. (1 Cor. 12:18)

In one of my kitchen drawers, I have an official church membership roll. It isn't our colorful, photo-filled church directory; it's a spreadsheet document that the clerk of session printed for us when we first came to the church. Each member takes up a row of neat cells that contain his or her name; status as a communicant or non-communicant; address; city, state, and zip; and phone number. The spreadsheet makes our church family look much tidier than it actually is. In reality, the people who are listed on this roll are complex individuals whose unique gifts and graces (and human weaknesses) can't be quantified in rigid columns and rows.

We may not be able to detail the members of our church adequately on a spreadsheet or even in our minds, but, as today's verse makes clear, the Lord can. He lovingly created "each one of them," knows them fully, and carefully placed them in the church for his glory. Elders' wives can gain confidence from this. The people sitting in the pews on Sunday morning are exactly the right people.

Particularly if our church is small, or is just starting out, it's tempting for us to think that we know exactly what kind of people it needs. We might look eagerly for families with young children who can fill the Sunday school classrooms, for people of color who can expand our witness in the community, or for someone with musical talents who can accompany the congregational singing. We might think that we definitely need either more young people or more mature Christians, more leaders or more helpers, more men or more women. And if we are committed to our personal ideals, we might be disappointed when we seem to get just the opposite.

But when we trust that a loving God has arranged each member in the body "as he chose," we can simply give thanks. The pastor who has extraordinary gifts and the awkward teenager in the back row both have a place in the church, according to God's perfect design. Each member has gifts that the church needs. Later in 1 Corinthians 12, Paul tells us that even the weaker members "are indispensable" (v. 22). Each member also needs the church. We are brought together in order to "have the same care for one another" (v. 25).

Not only is this an encouragement for us as we look out over the congregation, it is also an encouragement as we consider our own place in the assembly. Often it can be difficult for us to see how *we* fit in the local church. Our gifts don't seem quite right, and our sin struggles seem much too offensive, for us to belong. But the same Lord who carefully arranges every member in his church put you there for his own glory, too. Dear sister, take heart!

REFLECT. Why don't the people in your church always seem like a good fit for it? What criteria do we sometimes use to judge the "rightness" of church members? How does the truth that God himself arranges the members in his body encourage you as you serve the church?

PRAY. Thank the Lord for his kindness in specifically placing each member in your church. Ask him to lovingly add people to the church who are exactly right. Ask him to give you confidence in his choice of members.

ACT. Use your church directory (or official membership roll!) as a list for your daily prayers of thanksgiving. Each day, choose a name or two from the list and simply thank the Lord for creating them, giving them unique gifts and graces, and carefully placing them in your church body.

29. Your Elders Are Watching Out for You

Remember your leaders, those who spoke to you the word of God.... Obey your leaders and submit to them, for they are keeping watch over your souls, as those who will have to give an account. Let them do this with joy and not with groaning, for that would be of no advantage to you. (Heb. 13:7, 17)

On Sunday mornings, when I walk into the church building, most of the lights are off, and sometimes the main door is still locked. One room, however, is full of activity. In a small room at the end of a dark hallway, the elders—including my husband—gather for prayer. They lift up the congregation's concerns and ask the Lord to bless the worship of his people. They are there for the sake of Christ's church. They are there for me.

As an elder's wife, I can sometimes fall into the trap of thinking that elders' meetings are for the good of other people. Hurrying out the door so that my husband can make it to church in time for Sunday morning prayer doesn't always feel like it's good for me. Similarly, nights that I spend doing dishes alone, or singlehandedly wrangling kids, can give the impression that I'm serving our family while my husband is off serving other families. It can leave me wondering, "Who's going to care for *my* soul?" But today's verses remind me that elders have been given by Christ for the good of all his people—including the elders' wives.

The author of Hebrews tells us to "*remember* your leaders." Within the bustle of ministry life, we elders' wives shouldn't forget that we are sheep who are under the care of shepherds. We are just as much a part of what 1 Peter 5:2 calls "the flock of

God" as any other church member. This means that when the elders minister to the whole congregation, they are caring for us. Before God, they watch over our souls—knowing us, praying for us, ministering the Word to us, warning us against sin, and encouraging us toward Christlikeness. Our elders may have weaknesses and failings, and they don't always fulfill their calling as well as they should, but the efforts they make on our behalf are to our eternal "advantage" (Heb. 13:17). Every time they stand up in the congregation to pray or preach or read Scripture, they are doing good to our souls. Every time they meet to plan the curriculum for Sunday school or the details for an outreach event, or even to maintain the church membership roll, they are serving us.

As shepherds, elders serve the flock at the command of Christ, the Great Shepherd. After his ascension, he gave these men to the church as his gifts (see Eph. 4:8, 11). Just as Christ in heaven is ruling his kingdom and making intercession for his people, so his undershepherds are doing this work on earth. When you receive the admonition, care, and prayer of your elders, you receive the ministry of Christ.

REFLECT. What are some ways in which the elders of your church keep watch over your soul? How have you grown in your knowledge of the Lord because of their ministry? How have you been kept from sin? How are you more like Christ?

PRAY. "Remember your leaders," the writer of Hebrews exhorts us (13:7). Thank God for your elders by name. Pray for him to bless their labors and care for their souls. Ask him to encourage their hearts and make their work a joy.

Act. The next time your church elders have a meeting, take a minute to reflect on the fact that they are meeting for the sake of your soul.

30. The Blessing of Corporate Worship

I was glad when they said to me, "Let us go to
the house of the Lord!" (Ps. 122:1)

"Are you ready yet? We need to go. Now!" Every Sunday morning, no matter how carefully planned it is, always culminates in this last-minute dash for the door. Children scramble for church shoes; my husband snatches his sermon from our frequently unreliable printer; I double-check the settings on the slow cooker and quickly wipe toothpaste from the bathroom sink. With Bibles and bags flying, we tumble into the car and pull out of the driveway with seconds to spare.

Getting to church has never been easy. Today's verse comes from Psalm 122—one of the psalms of ascent that God's people would sing together as they traveled to Jerusalem for worship. The logistics of such a trip, which involved days on foot along dusty and dangerous roads, make our Sunday morning routines look leisurely. But the singers of this psalm were so captivated by the goal of their journey that they heard "Let's go!" with joy. Their desire to worship God ("to give thanks to the name of the Lord"—v. 4) in his presence (in "the house of the Lord"—vv. 1, 9) with his people ("the tribes [who] go up"—v. 4) motivated thousands of steps.

For us, too, the privilege of corporate worship can compel us to get out the door, even when it's not convenient. Our own commute to church doesn't lead to the physical city of Jerusalem, but it does take us to the heavenly one (see Heb. 12:22). In worship, we gather with saints and angels and Christ himself (see Heb. 12:22–24). We hear God speak to us in his Word, we sing songs that his people have sung for millennia, we join our hearts to the prayers that ascend to his throne, and we come to the Lord's table. In worship, we fellowship with our God.

It's interesting for elders' wives, in particular, to note that the call "Let us go to the house of the Lord" comes to the psalmist from the lips of others. Elders' wives are no strangers to other people's expectations, and chief among these may be the expectation that we will always be present for church worship services. We may sometimes view these obligations as being burdensome. But this verse holds up the congregational "Let's go" as a beautiful invitation. The psalmist receives the eager beckoning of his fellow worshipers with joy, because it's not merely the call of men—it's the call of the Lord. God himself is the one who tells us to gather for worship (see Heb. 10:24–25). Be there when you feel happy. Be there, as Christ himself was, when you are troubled (see Matt. 26:17–44). Be there when you are weary and when you are weak. There is no better place to be.

REFLECT. What sacrifices do you have to make in order to attend corporate worship? What does it cost you in terms of time, energy, or emotional resources?

PRAY. Using Psalm 122, ask the Lord to increase the delight you experience in church worship. Ask him to make you glad for the expectations of others (see v. 1) and the opportunity you have for gathering with his people (see v. 2). Give thanks for the worshipers whom God calls (see v. 4). Pray for the purity and peace of your local church—and of the church throughout the world (see vv. 6–9).

ACT. This Sunday morning, as you get ready for church, make your words "Let's go!" ones of joyful expectation. Whether you are coaxing children into coats or inviting visitors into the church building, cultivate and communicate delight for the privilege of worship.

31. Looking for the Heavenly Jerusalem

And I saw the holy city, new Jerusalem, coming down out of heaven from God, prepared as a bride adorned for her husband. (Rev. 21:2)

When I was a child, a family from our church demonstrated their gratitude for my dad's work as a pastor by allowing us to use their beach house for a much-needed vacation. After a several-hour car ride, we finally pulled in to the driveway and lugged our suitcases and groceries to the front door. As I remember it, we had no sooner turned the key in the lock than the phone in the house began to ring. My dad answered, and we all waited to hear who could be calling. It was one of the men from church, my dad reported with his hand cupped over the receiver: "He says the church ladies' room is out of toilet paper."

The caller was a notorious jokester, and his call was a prank; but that moment has become part of our family lore. Nothing illustrates the mundanity of life in an elder's family as clearly as being summoned from the beach to restock the church bathrooms. With its constant demands and repetitive practices, the local church is rarely a glamorous place to serve. Thankfully, today's verses remind us that the seeming insignificance of the present moment is only temporary. One day "soon" (Rev. 22:20), we will see the church revealed in its true glory. This future hope gives us strength for today.

The apostle John wrote the book of Revelation as he was enduring exile on the island of Patmos (see Rev. 1:9). His own Lord's Day worship was solitary and seemingly insignificant, and he addressed his letter to seven churches who were likewise scattered and suffering. It would have been easy for John to become discouraged, but the Lord gave him—and the churches he loved—a powerful encouragement.

Looking with compassion at John, the Lord invites him to join the worship of the heavenly places: "Come up here" (Rev. 4:1). In the midst of his suffering, John witnessed "a great multitude that no one could number, from every nation, from all tribes and peoples and languages, standing before the throne and before the Lamb" (Rev. 7:9). This would have encouraged John's heart, and it can encourage ours as well. In this life, we have the opportunity to join the saints and "innumerable angels in festal gathering" as we worship with our ordinary churches (Heb. 12:22). What's more, we look forward to that day in the age to come when the beauty of the church will be revealed and the church will be the perfect company of the redeemed, worshiping our God together forever.

REFLECT. What stories could you tell about the church's mundanity? What glimpses have you had of its true glory?

PRAY. Meditate on the beauty of the church in eternity: its multitude of members (see Rev. 7:9), its perfect construction and dimensions (see Rev. 21:9–21), its purity (see Rev. 21:27), its united songs of praise (see Rev. 5:9–14), and its light- and life-giving Savior (see Rev. 21:22–25). Ask the Lord to give you confidence in the promised future of the church and to enable you to love it well now.

ACT. When you are tempted to feel discouraged about your local church today, imagine what that church will be like in eternity. Picture the small attendance of an evening worship service increased to a multitude. Picture the tears of conflict and misunderstanding wiped away. Picture the sagging roof or tattered carpet replaced by beautiful craftsmanship with precious materials. Picture the half-hearted prayers or songs strengthened to a thunderous shout of praise. Then remember that Jesus promises that all of this will come true "soon" (Rev. 22:20).

CHALLENGES

32. When You Feel Like You Are Doing Everything

As a father shows compassion to his children, so the Lord shows compassion to those who fear him. For he knows our frame; he remembers that we are dust. (Ps. 103:13–14)

My friend was nearly in tears. "We have to set up for church and take down every week. Then I lead the singing while I also parent my kids. Nearly every evening, we have someone from the church showing up at our house with a pressing need for hospitality or counseling. We've had people spending the night on an almost constant rotation. And I'm teaching the women's Bible study." She ended with a sigh. "I'm just so tired."

Your own schedule might look different from my friend's, but you can probably relate to her. Whether we are juggling nursery duty with teaching Sunday school or hospitality with coffee-hour clean-up, elders' wives sometimes feel like we are doing everything. Even simply showing up to every worship service, outreach event, and baby shower can be a full-time job. Often, we are just so tired.

Thankfully, the Lord knows that. And in today's verses he reminds us that his disposition toward his overwhelmed and stressed-out people is compassion. In the parallel lines of verse 13, the Lord affirms that he regards us with tenderness—the same tenderness that a father shows to his beloved children. In fact, he shows us this tenderness because we *are* his children. We are the objects of his mercy, the recipients of his redemption, and the members of his family. When we feel like we can't do one more thing, he looks on us with love.

Verse 14 tells us that God shows us this compassion because he knows us. Our migraine headaches and meeting fatigue and skipped meals are not hidden from him. "He remembers that we are dust," the verse says. God is our creator; he literally made our first parents from dust (see Gen. 2:7). The psalmist also says that God "knows our frame." He knows it because he made it (see Ps. 139:13–16)—but also because he took our frame to himself. The creator of the universe became man—and so he is no stranger to hunger, thirst, and weariness. He knows what it is to hear, "Everyone is looking for you" (Mark 1:37) and to have to get up and go back to ministry. He can "sympathize with our weaknesses" (Heb. 4:15), because he himself has experienced all the trials and temptations of the life that we live as human beings.

Every day, we carry the hope of his gospel "in jars of clay, to show that the surpassing power belongs to God and not to us" (2 Cor. 4:7). As we go about our multitude of tasks, God uses even our human limitation to display his strength (see 2 Cor. 12:10).

REFLECT. Make a mental list of all the things that you do in the church. Does it feel manageable or overwhelming? How have you been comforted and strengthened by God during past seasons of busyness?

Pray. Read the words of Psalm 139 and make them your prayer. Praise God for knowing you, confess your inability to live apart from him, thank him for creating you, call on him to act justly in the world, and ask him to lead you in the path of everlasting life.

Act. God has compassionately given you other mature believers who can help you to see which tasks are essential for you to do and which could be eliminated or delegated to others. Talk to your husband or a trustworthy friend to get some perspective on what you should be doing in the church.

33. When You Feel Like You Aren't Doing Enough

For we are his workmanship, created in Christ Jesus
for good works, which God prepared beforehand,
that we should walk in them. (Eph. 2:10)

The coronavirus pandemic canceled everything. My calendar, which had previously displayed a matrix of appointments and events, was swept clean for the foreseeable future. For months, I left the house only once a week to go to the grocery store. Because of stay-at-home orders, I couldn't serve the church in any of my usual ways. I couldn't have people over for a meal or hug them on Sunday mornings. I couldn't visit elderly widows or hold new babies. I couldn't offer rides or childcare or companionship. I sat at home and felt like I wasn't doing enough.

It doesn't take a global crisis to bring on those feelings, of course. A variety of factors can limit the ability of an elder's wife to serve. Church dynamics, financial considerations, elderly parents, young children, outside employment, and health concerns can all impact our opportunities for service.

But the problem with feeling like we aren't doing enough is that this feeling focuses our hearts on ourselves. It causes us to marinate in our unreliable emotions, to measure ourselves against other people's capabilities, or to dwell on what we used to be able to do in the past. It burdens us with the assumption that others are disappointed in us. It fosters bitterness over our circumstances, and it creates resentment about our limitations. Ironically, such feelings often make us even *less* capable of serving well.

Thankfully, today's verse lifts our eyes off of ourselves and our circumstances and points us instead to the God who is sovereign over our opportunities for service. "We are his workmanship," Paul begins. We were created by him and redeemed by him. Every one of our limitations is known by him and falls under his sovereign design. You have exactly the gifts and the opportunities that he intended for you to have. He calls us to "good works" and knows our unique capacity for service. And even our good works themselves are under his control. He orchestrates the specific acts of service that we will do and prepares them "beforehand, that we should walk in them."

When our calendars don't display the amount or type of good works that we think we should be doing, we can look in faith to the Lord. Even seemingly small tasks find their significance when they are done unto him (see Col. 3:23). We take our allotted talents from his hand, use them diligently for his purposes, listen for his "Well done," and look ahead to that day when we will enter into his joy (see Matt. 25:14–30). We offer our service to him, and we rest in our identity in him. The One who made us and takes care of us is using us, in exactly the right ways, for his glory. As the Heidelberg Catechism teaches us to say, "I am not my own but belong with body and soul, both in life and in death, to my faithful Saviour Jesus Christ."

REFLECT. What limitations in your life cause you to do fewer (or different) good works than you would like to do?

PRAY. Confess to the Lord your sadness or bitterness over the current opportunities you have for service. Ask him to give you the grace to trust his sovereignty over your life.

ACT. Receive even seemingly minor opportunities for service (such as praying or giving encouragement) as God's good will for you. Give thanks that you are able to serve him in exactly the way that he intended.

34. When You Are Home Alone—Again

Therefore when we could bear it no longer, we were willing to be left behind at Athens alone, and we sent Timothy, our brother and God's coworker in the gospel of Christ, to establish and exhort you in your faith, that no one be moved by these afflictions. (1 Thess. 3:1–3)

Nineteenth-century preacher Charles Spurgeon was extraordinarily busy in ministry. For thirty-eight years, frequent preaching engagements took him away from his home for long periods of time. In the early days of their marriage, his wife Susannah would often cry when he had to leave. Years later, she recalled a conversation that finally shifted her perspective. "Wifey," Charles said to her, "... don't you see, you are giving me to God, in letting me go to preach the gospel to poor sinners?'" After that, she sought to send Charles off with joy and to release him to God as her sacrifice.

Elders' wives have to sacrifice their husbands in dozens of ways. We give up our demands on their time to elders' meetings, home visits, and sermon or Bible-study preparation—which often come at the end of an already long work day. We give up our demands on their attention to text messages, phone calls, and a long line of people who are waiting for them after church. We give up our demands on their emotional energy to what Paul calls "the daily pressure. . . [of] anxiety for all the churches" (2 Cor. 11:28). Sometimes it's enough to make you want to cry.

Although the apostle Paul was unmarried, he too knew the pain of giving up a beloved companion for the sake of the gospel. In today's verses, he writes about his decision to be "left behind at Athens alone" so that Timothy could serve the church. Timothy was probably dearer to Paul than anyone else was. Paul describes him as his "brother" (see, for instance, 2 Cor. 1:1) and his "child" (see, for instance, 1 Cor. 4:17). Repeatedly he calls Timothy "beloved" (1 Cor. 4:17; 2 Tim. 1:2). He tells the Philippian church that he has "no one like him" (Phil. 2:20). For Paul, to be "left behind . . . alone" without Timothy was to be alone indeed.

And yet Paul willingly made this sacrifice, because he set his heart on something more precious than his own comfort. He knew that Timothy did not ultimately belong to him but was "God's coworker in the gospel of Christ." Timothy was not created to serve Paul; he was created to serve God. What's more, the church of Christ—and particularly the church under affliction—moved Paul's heart. He gave up Timothy to "establish and exhort" the Thessalonians so that they would not fall away during their sufferings (1 Thess. 3:2). Paul's loneliness meant that God's people would not have to struggle alone.

Dear sister, your long nights in a dark house, Sundays alone in the pew, and rescheduled anniversary dinners are not insignificant. They are sacrifices you are making for Christ and his kingdom, and they are precious to our Lord.

REFLECT. In what ways do you have to give up your claims on your husband's time, attention, and emotional energy? How have you struggled with doing this?

PRAY. Using today's verses, give thanks for the opportunities you have for sacrificing for the sake of the gospel. Ask the Lord to make you "willing to be left behind . . . alone."

ACT. With the examples of Susannah Spurgeon and the apostle Paul in mind, seek the Holy Spirit's help to respond with joy (a smile, a hug, a word of encouragement) as your husband leaves the home this week.

35. When You Face Unjust Criticism

"For John came neither eating nor drinking,
and they say, 'He has a demon.' The Son of Man came
eating and drinking, and they say, 'Look at him! A glutton
and a drunkard, a friend of tax collectors and sinners!'
Yet wisdom is justified by her deeds." (Matt. 11:18–19)

Gloria Furman, a pastor's wife in the Arabian Peninsula, tells the
story of a woman in her church who came up and said to her, "So
many times you have disappointed me and do not work to please
me as my pastor's wife." Perhaps you have a similar story of your
own. Even if it's couched in less direct language, elders' wives can
receive criticism for everything from the length of our hair to
the length of our husbands' sermons. The way we use our time,
our money, and our homes; the choices we make about how and
where to serve; and the outward conduct of our children are all
seemingly fair game for congregational critique. What's more,
our beloved husbands can be the public targets of uncharitable
words and unfair commentary—and we feel the sting deeply.

But when elders and their wives are the objects of unjust
criticism from God's people, they are not alone. Today's verses
remind us that both John the Baptist and Jesus faced nearly
constant criticism during their ministries. The sinless God-man
and the preacher who was the greatest human ever born (see
Luke 7:28) were both relentlessly berated. As Matthew Henry
wrote regarding these verses, "The most unspotted innocency,
and the most unparalleled excellency, will not always be a fence
against the reproach of tongues." If we have sinned, we should

accept the justly deserved criticism and repent. But we should also know that even exemplary conduct won't exempt us from critique.

Perhaps counterintuitively, this should encourage us. Elsewhere, Jesus spurs his disciples to gospel boldness by reminding them that reviling and false accusations are a perennial feature of kingdom work and an opportunity for us to strengthen our assurance: "Rejoice and be glad . . . for so they persecuted the prophets who were before you" (Matt. 5:12). If we are wrongly criticized, then we are in good company.

Gloria's story had a happy ending. Her critic went on to say, "And now I'm beginning to realize that you are not here to please me. All of us exist to please the Lord." This is the happy ending we can all look for—whether or not our critics ever recognize it. John the Baptist and Jesus both had unique ministries that received unique complaints, yet they took a shared hope from the ultimate vindication they would receive from an all-wise God. They lived to please him, and they looked for their reward from him. They labored boldly in the callings and circumstances they had received, embodying the spirit of Paul's later words "So, whether you eat or drink, or whatever you do, do all to the glory of God" (1 Cor. 10:31).

REFLECT. When have you or your husband received criticism regarding your ministry? What was your response to it?

PRAY. Read Matthew 5:44–45: "Love your enemies and pray for those who persecute you, so that you may be sons of your Father who is in heaven." Ask the Lord to give you love for your critics as you pray for their spiritual good.

ACT. Whenever you make a choice this week that might draw criticism, focus on living before the face of God, seeking to please him, and working with your whole heart regardless of what others think (see Col. 3:22).

36. When Church Members Clash

I entreat Euodia and I entreat Syntyche to agree in the
Lord. Yes, I ask you also, true companion, help these
women, who have labored side by side with me in the gospel
together with Clement and the rest of my fellow workers,
whose names are in the book of life. (Phil. 4:2–3)

The Philippian church began well. Under Paul's ministry, a prominent businesswoman and faithful prayer-meeting attendee came to Christ along with her whole family (see Acts 16:13–15). She was soon joined by a girl who had been set free from her demons (see vv. 16–18) and a corrections officer who, along with his family, was both hospitable and joyful (see vv. 32–34). From the moment of its first assembly, this little church committed itself to the spread of the gospel (see Phil. 1:5, 27–30). But it was not a perfectly peaceful church. Paul starts the fourth chapter of his letter to Philippi with these words: "I entreat Euodia and I entreat Syntyche to agree in the Lord" (v. 2).

Like many of our churches, the Philippian church experienced congregational conflict. We don't know the source of the trouble between Euodia and Syntyche. Was it the church budget? The way they were each educating their children? Their convictions about eschatology? Their desires for certain styles of worship music?

Did they argue because of personality or preference or principle? Whatever their issue was, it was affecting the entire congregation. In language that assumed that everyone knew the situation, Paul called out their disagreement in a public letter and added an appeal to church leaders to help them resolve it.

Perhaps you are familiar with the whole-church turmoil that conflict between members can cause. What begins as a matter of conviction spills over into anger, selfishness, and unkindness. Gossip and factions aren't far behind. It twists my stomach in knots just thinking about it.

Thankfully, Paul demonstrates three priorities that we should have as we navigate such storms. First, he focuses on Christ. Rather than take sides, he calls the women to "agree in the Lord." When church life gets tense, we can be quick to align ourselves with one person or the other. Instead, because of our union with Christ, we must seek alignment with the Lord. Next, Paul acknowledges the dignity and value of the arguing believers. It's easy to think dismissively of church members who are acting abrasively, but Paul reminds us that Euodia and Syntyche (as well as the people in our own churches) are our fellow workers in the cause of the gospel and have souls secured by Christ's blood. Finally, Paul acts with gospel optimism. By asking his "true companion" to intervene, he demonstrates his confidence that conflicts in the church can be resolved. The Lord delights in unity among his people (see Ps. 133:1–2), and his Spirit can change hearts and minds. As church leaders—often, our own husbands—work for peace, we can live in the hope that the Lord will give it.

REFLECT. Think of a conflict that is taking place in your church. Which of Paul's three priorities are you apt to forget as you consider the situation? What happens when you don't think biblically about conflict?

PRAY. Read Psalm 133. Ask the Lord to bring peace and unity to his church, because it is good and he says it pleases him: "Behold, how good and pleasant it is when brothers dwell in unity! It is like the precious oil on the head, running down on the beard, on the beard of Aaron, running down on the collar of his robes!" (Ps. 133:1–2).

ACT. Put Paul's priorities into practice as you encounter church conflict. Keep Christ in focus. Remind yourself of other believers' true identity. Cultivate hope.

37. When People Leave the Church

And there arose a sharp disagreement, so that they
separated from each other. Barnabas took Mark with
him and sailed away to Cyprus. (Acts 15:39)

I can think of three ways that people leave the church. When people are moving away, they leave accompanied by a cake-and-punch reception in the fellowship hall. We exchange hugs; we pray; we cry. We give them a gift and ask them to keep in touch. We express our hope of seeing them again. In other situations, people grow old or sick, and they leave with a funeral. We hug their family members; we pray; we cry. We give thanks for their life. We anticipate seeing them again at the resurrection. Neither of these are easy goodbyes. But the worst are the times when we can't mark people's leaving. One Sunday, their familiar faces are in the third row on the left, and the next Sunday, they aren't. Maybe there was a tense elders' meeting or a long phone call during the week. Maybe there was a church discipline case. Maybe there wasn't. Sometimes people just leave. And we don't know whether we'll see them again.

All three kinds of partings appear in the New Testament. On the beach at Tyre, they may not have served cake and punch, but the church prayed, cried, and hugged and kissed Paul as they took him to his departing ship (see Acts 20:36–38; 21:5–6). In Joppa, after the death of a godly woman, her weeping congregation displayed the clothes that she had made for them (see Acts 9:36–39). But in Antioch, Barnabas and John Mark left Paul over "a sharp disagreement." These three departures remind us that churches have always had to say goodbye to their members. In this life, the time we spend together always has an expiration date, and hard goodbyes are not uncommon. These stories also affirm that, just as the Lord specifically noted the sorrow that was felt by these early believers, he marks our own tears over church departures . As the psalmist wrote, "You have . . . put my tears in your bottle. Are they not in your book?" (Ps. 56:8).

Today's verses about Barnabas and Paul, in particular, can strengthen our hearts when people leave our churches under hard circumstances. For one thing, this text acknowledges that relationships in the church can be complicated. It's not clear who was right and who was wrong about John Mark—it's clear only that the matter couldn't be easily resolved. In the same way, if people leave your church, it isn't necessarily because you or the church have failed in some way. This text also gives us hope. Yes, the two parties separated ways. Yes, this was difficult. But, in the end, it served the good of the kingdom as the Lord multiplied gospel proclamation throughout the region. What's more, this story doesn't conclude in the book of Acts. Years later, Paul wrote, "Get Mark and bring him with you, for he is very useful to me for ministry" (2 Tim. 4:11). A painful parting of ways today may resolve itself in love a few years later. And, between Christians, it will certainly resolve in eternity.

REFLECT. Have you experienced each of the three kinds of partings that are described here? What makes each kind difficult?

PRAY. Express to the Lord the sorrow that you feel over departures from your church. Ask him to remind you that he will one day "wipe away tears from all faces" (Isa. 25:8).

ACT. Think of someone who left your church without a goodbye. Pray for them today. Ask the Lord to use them wherever he takes them. Look expectantly for God to bring you back together with them—in this life or in the next.

COMMUNITY

JOYS

38. You Will Rejoice

He who goes out weeping, bearing the seed for sowing, shall come home with shouts of joy, bringing his sheaves with him. (Ps. 126:6)

The joke that elders' families actually live at the church building exposes a kernel of truth. Of all the people in the congregation, we are often the most likely to be the first to arrive and the last to leave. When the doors are open, we're there. In the book of Luke, we read about another godly woman who was always at church. Anna "did not depart from the temple, worshiping with fasting and prayer night and day" (Luke 2:37). And her daily labor resulted in a sweet reward. After faithfully showing up in the right place at the right time, Anna was one of the first people to see the object of all true worship come into the place of worship. When Mary and Joseph carried baby Jesus into the temple, Anna's years of constant prayer were answered. She saw the fulfillment of God's promises with her own eyes, and she "[gave] thanks to God" (Luke 2:38).

As the days and nights of our own lives are taken up by kingdom work, we too can look forward to a future day of rejoicing when we will see with our own eyes the redeeming work of God.

Today's verse comes from the psalms of ascent—songs that the people of God would sing on their way to the house of God. It highlights both the hard work and the promised joy of laboring in God's field. First, the psalmist acknowledges that sowing gospel seed is not easy. It's constant work, and, often, it's discouraging work. Our husbands go out to preach, week after week, seeing little visible fruit. We speak to our unbelieving neighbors repeatedly, and they still shrug Jesus off. We plead with our children to come to Christ, but they don't seem to give their sin a backward glance. The sower, as one translation says, "continually goes forth weeping" (NKJV).

But that's not the end of the story. At the end of the season, the laborer doesn't trudge back from the fields empty-handed, his head hanging low. He "come[s] home with shouts of joy, bringing his sheaves with him." Although our faithful planting and watering may bear little obvious fruit during this life, we can trust that "God . . . gives the growth" (1 Cor. 3:7). The One who delights to save is even now working in the secret places (see Mark 4:26–27). The "smallest of all seeds" will grow into a great tree (Matt. 13:32; see also v. 31), and we will come home at last with rejoicing.

REFLECT. Think about a time when your kingdom labors have born visible fruit—perhaps a time when someone came to faith in Christ or obviously deepened their knowledge of him. How did you respond when this happened? Imagine the joy of that one instance being multiplied at the end of days!

PRAY. Make a list of a few unbelievers whose salvation you desire. Ask the Lord to give you opportunities to plant gospel seeds or water gospel truth within them (see 1 Cor. 3:6). Ask him to grant you the joy of witnessing their profession of faith.

ACT. The next time you have to be at church—again!—resolve to show up with expectation rather than grumbling. You will be in one of the very best places to see the fruit of God's redeeming work.

39. You Are a Light

"You are the light of the world. . . . Let your light shine before others, so that they may see your good works and give glory to your Father who is in heaven." (Matt. 5:14, 16)

Belshazzar the Babylonian king was terrified. In the middle of his blasphemous, idolatrous, drunken revel, a hand appeared on his palace wall and wrote three strange words (see Dan. 5:1–5, 25). The king's face blanched, his legs wobbled, and his knees knocked (see v. 6). *What could this mean?* Thankfully, his queen had an idea. Entering the banquet hall, she suggested they call Daniel, the all-but-forgotten wise man from the days of Nebuchadnezzar. When Daniel arrived, Belshazzar addressed him. "I have heard of you that the spirit of the gods is in you, and that light and understanding and excellent wisdom are found in you" (Dan. 5:14). The pagan king didn't understand Daniel or his God, but he recognized that Daniel had *something* that might illuminate Belshazzar's confusing situation.

In our communities, we regularly interact with befuddled and even terrified people. Our neighbors worry aloud that their children are making bad choices and that their spouses are being unfaithful. Our coworkers set their hearts on the uncertainty of riches and visibly wobble with every report from the stock market. Our doctors and hair stylists wryly acknowledge that they fix people for a living while their own lives haven't turned out the way that they planned. Like Belshazzar, they tell us their troubles because they realize that we have *something*—"the spirit of the gods," perhaps—that might give them comfort and clarity.

In today's verses, Jesus encourages us to make gospel use of such opportunities. "You are the light of the world," he tells his gathered disciples. Just like the lights of LA or New York City, which are visible even from space, you are going to be noticed when you live a Spirit-filled life. Just like the lamp on your nightstand that enables you to read this page, you help people to see clearly what's in front of their faces. Because Christ dwells in you, you sparkle within this "crooked and twisted generation" (Phil. 2:15), and its confused people look to you for illumination. Your acts of kindness and generosity, the thoughtful attention you give to the outcast and overlooked, your determination to be holy when no one else gives it a thought—all of these will be highly visible. And all of them give you a chance to reveal spiritual truth.

Of course, neither Daniel nor the disciples shone with light of their own making. Like Moses's face, brilliant with the reflected light of God's glory (see Ex. 34:29), we are radiant only because our Lord is even more radiant. And as our friends and coworkers seek us out, we invite them to give glory to God alone.

REFLECT. How have you made good use of your opportunities for shedding light? How do you need the Spirit's help to shine boldly?

PRAY. Read Phil. 2:14–16. Confess ways in which your sin has dimmed the light you should be shining. Ask God to forgive you and enable you to be "blameless and innocent." Ask him for help with "holding fast to the word of life." Ask him to make you a bright light in a dark world.

ACT. Think of someone who may give you an opportunity to shine gospel light this week. Maybe a janitor regularly shares her financial troubles or a fellow soccer mom often seems eager for parenting advice. Prayerfully consider how you can point her to Christ when this happens.

40. God Loves to Save

"For this is the will of my Father, that everyone who looks
on the Son and believes in him should have eternal life,
and I will raise him up on the last day." (John 6:40)

A few years ago, a member of our church gave us a set of boards for playing cornhole—a lawn game in which players get points by throwing beanbags through a hole in a wooden board. I enjoy playing cornhole, but I'm not good at it. Thankfully, my teenage son usually chooses me to play on his team, and he is very good. Most of my beanbags fly wide of the board and land on the grass or narrowly miss my son's head. His slide effortlessly up the slope and *plop* into the hole, exactly as planned. If I played cornhole by myself, I'd be defeated every time. But because my son plays with me, I can step onto the grass confident of victory.

When it comes to evangelism, I suspect most us feel that our gospel efforts generally fly wide of the mark. We speak to our child about the importance of forsaking sin and trusting Christ, and she toddles off to steal a toy from her sister. We explain biblical truth to our coworkers and neighbors, and they stare uncomfortably into their coffee mugs. We appeal to elderly relatives to consider their need for salvation, and they pick up the remote to change the channel. For elders' wives, watching our husbands' efforts can compound our temptations to be discouraged. Week after week, they teach evangelistic Bible studies, preach evangelistic sermons, and engage unbelievers through the ministry of the church— and each toss seems to land with a thud on the lawn. Thankfully, today's verse reminds us that we are not doing the work of evangelism alone and that the salvation of others does not depend on us.

Christ's words in John 6 encourage us in two important ways. First, they remind us that God loves to save. The salvation of his people is "the will of [the] Father." It's what brings him glory. It's what he delights to do. Peter asserts this truth from another angle: "The Lord . . . is patient toward you, not wishing that any should perish, but that all should reach repentance" (2 Peter 3:9). When we desire that unbelievers be saved, we want what God wants. This gives our evangelistic labors significance. When we proclaim Christ to a lost and dying world, we align our efforts with the will of the Father.

Second, this verse reminds us that the results of our gospel work are in the Lord's sovereign hand. It is *God* who wills salvation, who grants eternal life, who raises people up on the last day. Our feeble efforts could never save anyone, but God's sovereignty means that "all that the Father gives [Christ] will come to [him]" and that he will "lose nothing" (John 6:37, 39). Our conversations with unbelievers who are enslaved to sin and death often seem to accomplish little. But those conversations are what God will use to call the elect to himself, and on the final day not one person will be missing.

REFLECT. When do your evangelistic labors (or the evangelistic labors of your husband) seem to fly wide? When have you seen God's hand at work despite your feeble efforts?

PRAY. Think of an unbeliever whom you desire to come to faith. Ask the Lord to grant this person salvation. Ask him to use your evangelistic efforts to accomplish his perfect will.

ACT. Resolve to approach your gospel conversations this week with hope. Remember that God loves to save. Remember that he is sovereign over salvation.

41. Partners in the Gospel

I thank my God in all my remembrance of you, always
in every prayer of mine for you all making my prayer
with joy, because of your partnership in the gospel
from the first day until now. (Phil. 1:3–5)

Yesterday, my to-do list was full of mundane tasks. I scrubbed the dishes and did the laundry. I cooked. I cleaned. I logged hours at work. I spent time with two women from church. I attended midweek Bible study. I took the kids and their friends to the pool and supplied them with snacks. I prayed. I read the Bible. I made sure my husband had clean socks. I exercised. It was an ordinary day. And it didn't always feel like important kingdom work.

In today's verses, though, Paul affirms the value of the unseen and unglamorous work done by ordinary Christians. The great apostle Paul, who planted churches throughout the known world, looked at the members of the congregation in Philippi and called them his partners in the gospel. This is true of everyone who gives support to kingdom workers. As elders' wives, we often stay home while our husbands go out. We often do the invisible and unacknowledged work while our husbands do the public work. We often take the supporting roles while our husbands take the leading roles. But in the economy of the kingdom, the work of elders' wives is essential.

As we survey Paul's letter to the Philippians, we notice that this church partnered with his gospel work in three important ways: they lived lives that were worthy of the gospel, they prayed at all times, and they provided for Paul's material needs. So, too, elders' wives come alongside their husbands through these vital tasks. First, we seek to live "worthy of the gospel of Christ" (Phil. 1:27). With the help of the Holy Spirit, we behave in a way that is shaped by the gospel and that therefore promotes the gospel. Having a godly wife encourages our husbands—and their ministries. Next, we pray for gospel success. Paul faithfully prayed for the Philippians, and he knew they prayed for him (see Phil. 1:3–4, 19). Elsewhere, he invited the church at Rome to "strive together with me in your prayers" (Rom. 15:30). When we pray for our husbands, we are striving with them in important kingdom work—even if we never leave home. Finally, we provide for their material needs. The Philippians "entered into partnership with [Paul] in giving and receiving" (Phil. 4:15), which allowed him to devote himself to gospel ministry. When elders' wives cook meals, fix leaky faucets, or contribute income, we enable our husbands' ministry.

The partnership that we have in the gospel alongside our husbands has two important results. First, it gives our husbands joy.

Just as Paul was able to pray "with joy" for his Philippian partners, our husbands' hearts can be lightened by our largely unseen work on their behalf. And, most importantly, our partnership brings glory to God. As they receive our ministry to them, our husbands will have an opportunity to echo Paul's words of thanks to God for the gift that God has given them.

REFLECT. What mundane tasks make up your days? In what way are these tasks nevertheless important kingdom work?

PRAY. Thank God for someone who has encouraged *you* in your labors as an elder's wife. Ask God to give you opportunities to encourage your husband in his own work.

ACT. As you cross items off your to-do list for today, remember that you are a vital partner in the gospel.

42. Revive Us, O Lord!

On your walls, O Jerusalem, I have set watchmen; all the day and all the night they shall never be silent. You who put the Lord in remembrance, take no rest, and give him no rest until he establishes Jerusalem and makes it a praise in the earth. (Isa. 62:6–7)

Most elders' wives have no shortage of good things we could do in the world. The homeless shelter always needs toiletries and canned goods. The pregnancy care center needs volunteer counselors. The local school needs classroom aides. The library needs volunteers for the book sale, the town garden committee needs hands for highway cleanup day, and the Little League could certainly use a few more dugout moms. Any of these could be a valuable way for us to contribute. But the most important way we can serve the world around us is largely invisible. It's unlikely to show up on the town website. It won't merit a line on your resume. In fact, most people will never know that you are doing it.

Today's verses, which come from the prophet Isaiah, make it clear that one of the most important things we can be doing is praying. Isaiah calls all "who put the Lord in remembrance" to come before God and plead for him to strengthen and increase his church (to "establish . . . Jerusalem") and make it "a praise in the earth." Jerusalem was the place of God's dwelling and the locus of true worship. When the Israelites asked God to make it "a praise in the earth," they were asking him to draw people from all nations who would worship him rightly in his presence. As God's people, we should follow this pattern by praying for the well-being of the church and the spiritual awakening of people in our communities and around the world.

Isaiah's words remind us that prayer is constant, hard work. Just as the watchmen of Jerusalem never get a vacation and instead proclaim God's truth "all the day and all the night" to whomever will listen, so the praying people of God don't schedule days off, either. They "take no rest and give [God] no rest" as they ask him to pour out his Spirit in their midst and give his Word success. Praying for revival is difficult, uncomfortable, invisible work. If we pray "without ceasing" (1 Thess. 5:17), we should expect to be tired.

The hard work of prayer would seem foolish, then, if it weren't for the promises that God attaches to it. God "set watchmen" on the walls—giving pastors and teachers and apostles to his church (see Eph. 4:11)—and he pledges to answer his people's prayers by establishing his kingdom and exalting its King. Although our prayers seem weak and insignificant now, God's promises will not fail. People throughout the world will hear the words of salvation and flee to Christ. Unbelievers will notice the church's loveliness and long to join in its worship. One day, our constant work of prayer will receive its glorious answer. And, one day, we will rejoice.

REFLECT. What are some ways in which you regularly do good in the world? Do you think of prayer as a service to unbelievers? Why or why not?

PRAY. Using the words of Psalm 85, ask the Lord to grant revival to the church and world. Ask him to forgive sins and pour out his Spirit. Ask him to make your community, in particular, a place where "faithfulness springs up from the ground" (v. 11).

ACT. As you have opportunities for serving unbelievers in tangible ways this week, make sure you also take time to pray that they will come to know and love the Lord.

43. The Lord Will Wipe Away Every Tear

He will swallow up death forever; and the Lord God will wipe
away tears from all faces, and the reproach of his people he will
take away from all the earth, for the Lord has spoken. (Isa. 25:8)

Sara was young, beautiful, creative, and personable. She loved children and dogs and painting abstract canvases. She was a sincere believer and a member of our small church. She was my friend. She was also an opioid addict. Over the years, in a series of waves, her battles with mental health issues and addiction crested and subsided. Sometimes she was sitting in her usual pew and dressed in her Sunday best. Sometimes she was on the streets and no one could find her. Eventually, her struggles overcame her, and Sara took her own life.

Every week, we worship and work alongside people whose lives are plagued with significant complications. Marriage problems, addiction, mental health issues, trauma, and a myriad of other trials present long-term challenges that they may not be able to resolve. For elders and their wives, who are often the ones offering emergency shelter, supporting caregivers, or leading repeated interventions, it can seem like the struggle with brokenness and sin is a losing one. Our hearts overflow with compassion for our hurting friends, and it never feels like we've done enough for them. Year after year, the complexities of their situations only evolve into fresh problems. We hold the hands of suffering people, and we groan, "How long, O Lord?" (Ps. 13:1).

Thankfully, today's verse lifts our eyes to the glorious future of all God's people—no matter how weighed down they are in this life. Here, Isaiah declares that pain and sorrow have an expiration date. One day, God will "swallow up death forever" and will "wipe away tears from all faces." The trials that now seize so much time and energy will be gone—taken away in an instant by a sovereign act of our gracious God. One day, he will also gather up every shame and take it "away from all the earth." The sins that threaten to crush his people with their ugly persistence will be nowhere to be found—they will be cast "as far as the east is from the west" (Ps. 103:12). On that day, God's people will be lovely, radiant, orderly, beautiful, bright, pure, and perfect (see Rev. 21:9–27). They will "see his face, and his name will be on their foreheads" (Rev. 22:4). All sorrow and sighing will flee away, and the redeemed will come in to Zion with singing (see Isa. 35:10).

When troubles press in and don't let up, it can be tempting for us to think that this heavenly vision sounds too good to be true. But it isn't. Isaiah concludes his prophesy of this future restoration with the only guarantee we need: "For the Lord has spoken" (Isa. 25:8). Take heart. We have a powerful and loving God, and he will accomplish it.

REFLECT. What burden are you currently bearing that seems to have no solution? Why is this situation particularly discouraging to you?

PRAY. Think of a difficult situation in your church or community. Bring it before the Lord. Confess your inclination to "grow weary in doing good" (2 Thess. 3:13). Ask for the Spirit to help you persevere. Ask him to help you to trust that "the Lord has spoken."

ACT. This week, as you provide support and resources to hurting people—some of whom have problems that may not resolve during this life—remind yourself that, one day, the Lord will answer your prayers by wiping away "tears from all faces." Lift up your head, and give thanks.

CHALLENGES

44. When You Suffer

"In the world you will have tribulation. But take heart;
I have overcome the world." (John 16:33)

When my husband was in seminary, we lived in a condominium owned by the school. Almost all our neighbors were seminary students and their families. Predictably, many of us struggled to make ends meet, and the run-down vehicles parked out front testified to the community's general financial strain. One night, a thief entered the complex and stole our neighbor's car. Rather than accelerating the criminal's getaway, however, the car broke down before he could exit the neighborhood, and the thief had to abandon it in the middle of the road.

We still laugh about that story and retell it at dinner parties when the occasion fits, but it also makes me a little sad. The car's owner was faithfully trying to prepare for gospel ministry, and he seemed to get nothing but trouble in return. Maybe that has been your experience as an elder's wife. The oven breaks the day you are hosting church visitors. Your kids come down with a stomach bug late Saturday night. You plan to start a Bible study but can't find a time when everyone can come.

Your life seems to be filled with discouragement, conflict, and opposition.

Dear sister, the Lord is not ignorant of your suffering, and his Word does not dismiss it. In fact, the Bible tells us repeatedly that we are to expect suffering. "In the world you will have tribulation," says Jesus (John 16:33). He spoke these words to his disciples—the ones he would shortly send out into the world to plant churches in his name. Like our own families, the disciples gave their lives to the cause of Christ. And, like our families, they experienced trouble. Hebrews 11 tells us that God's messengers throughout redemptive history have been "destitute, afflicted, mistreated" (v. 37). For those who serve Christ, suffering is certain.

But Jesus also gave courage to his disciples, and he gives us courage as well: "Take heart," he says. "I have overcome the world." We may not be able to avoid suffering, but, as Christians, we can go beyond simply enduring it—beyond gritting our teeth and waiting for the next vacation or paycheck. We can look for our Redeemer to redeem our troubles for his glory. "We rejoice in our sufferings," Paul says, "knowing that suffering produces endurance, and endurance produces character, and character produces hope, and hope does not put us to shame, because God's love has been poured into our hearts through the Holy Spirit who has been given to us" (Rom. 5:3–5). The Lord is sovereign over leaking roofs and skeptical in-laws. He has designed them for our good, and he promises to give us the Holy Spirit to help us. We can, alongside Paul, greet troubles with rejoicing, because we know that they will bear spiritual fruit in our hearts.

REFLECT. In what ways have you suffered during your time as an elder's wife? How have your sufferings produced endurance, character, and hope in your heart?

PRAY. Using the words of Psalm 13, bring your suffering before the Lord. Tell him about your sorrow (see vv. 1–2). Ask him to help you (see vv. 3–4). Confess the truth of his steadfast love toward you (see vv. 5–6).

ACT. One of the most uncomfortable aspects of suffering is how weak it makes us feel. Post these words of Christ where they can encourage you: "My grace is sufficient for you, for my power is made perfect in weakness" (2 Cor. 12:9).

45. When You Are Weary in the Workplace

As for you, brothers, do not grow weary
in doing good. (2 Thess. 3:13)

The Thessalonian church, like most churches, was a complicated group of people. Paul held them up as an exemplary congregation and observed that they had spurred others to faithfulness with their own faithfulness (see 1 Thess. 1:7–8). And yet some of the members were still confused about what they should be doing with their time. Paul noted that some "walk in idleness, not busy at work, but busybodies" (2 Thess. 3:11). If "some" had quit their jobs, it's reasonable to assume that others were obediently imitating Paul's diligent labors in the workplace and the ministry (see 2 Thess. 3:7–9). They probably felt more than a little tired.

For elders and elders' wives who hold jobs in addition to ministry responsibilities, their workload can be wearying. Bible study preparation, hospitality, and discipleship all have to happen after hours or be squeezed into a lunch break. Work places significant demands on our energy and time, and ministry seems to gobble up whatever is left. When we feel overwhelmed, we may be quick to contrast our own labors with the seeming idleness of other people. It is also easy for us to see ourselves as hapless victims of our jobs' demands. Sometimes, like the idle Thessalonians, we'd just like to quit working altogether.

In today's verse, Paul offers encouragement to work-weary Christians. With his expansive command, "do good," he dignifies all kinds of work. We "do good" in the church, and we "do good" when we show up every Monday morning to an office or jobsite. And the value of our work gives us energy to keep going. Through our hard work, we earn money to provide for our own needs (see 2 Thess. 3:8, 10, 12). Paul did this—he labored both in ministry and as a tentmaker to earn his own living so he wouldn't be "a burden" to the church (v. 8). Our work is good for others as well. Not only does it keep us from depending on other people's resources, it also allows us to be generous to "anyone in need" (Eph. 4:28). The time we spend in the workplace may also yield opportunities for us to care for our coworkers. Joseph did good to his employer Pharaoh and to the people of Egypt by preparing them to face the coming famine (see Gen. 41:46–49, 53–54). The servant girl did good to her master Naaman by pointing him to the true God (see 2 Kings 5:2–3). Work is not a meaningless slog; it is "doing good."

Most importantly, 2 Thessalonians 3 reminds us that God values our work. By exhorting the believers to "do their work quietly" (v. 12), Paul acknowledges that good work doesn't always result in public fanfare. Sometimes the Lord is the only one who sees that we are "busy at work" (v. 11). It's not easy to resolve questions about how we should best spend our limited time and energy, but we can be confident that our hard work pleases God (see vv. 6–7, 10, 12). We labor at the Lord's command, for his glory, and with the help of his Spirit.

Do not grow weary.

REFLECT. What are the work responsibilities that you and your husband juggle during a week? When are you most tempted to "grow weary" and give up?

PRAY. Read Colossians 3:23–24. Thank God for giving you work that glorifies him. Confess times when you have failed to "work heartily." Ask the Lord for the strength to serve him well. Thank him for his promised reward.

ACT. Paul's own hard work was an example and an encouragement to the Thessalonians. As you go to work today, remember that your example can help others to see the value of their own work before God.

46. When You Long for Friends

Do your best to come to me soon. (2 Tim. 4:9)

The apostle Paul was no wimp. He defended the faith before kings (see Acts 26), wrote much of the New Testament, planted numerous churches, suffered extended imprisonment, and endured beatings and shipwrecks (see 2 Cor. 11:25). We'd describe him as intelligent, persistent, and hardy. Since he had that kind of character, it might be tempting for us to think of him as someone who didn't really need other people and who certainly didn't need friends. But we would be wrong.

Repeatedly in Scripture, the apostle Paul expresses a longing to be with various saints in the churches (see, for instance, 1 Cor. 16:7; Phil. 2:23–24; 1 Thess. 2:17). He earnestly prayed that God would permit him to be physically present with his friends (see Rom. 1:9–15), and he encouraged church members to cultivate affectionate relationships with one another (see, for instance, Rom. 16:16). As today's verse demonstrates, Timothy was Paul's particular friend, and Paul especially wanted to see him. In some of his last recorded words, Paul writes to Timothy, "Do your best to come to me soon" (2 Tim. 4:9) and then, just a few verses later, "Do your best to come before winter" (v. 21).

Life in ministry can sometimes leave us feeling friendless. You may be in a church with people who already seem to have plenty of friends—or with whom you have little in common. The role you fill as an elder's wife might make people reluctant to befriend you—or eager to befriend you for the wrong reasons. Difficult circumstances within the church may have even cost you friends.

In 2 Timothy 4, we read that Paul's friends abandoned him when he needed them most: "At my first defense no one came to stand by me, but all deserted me" (v. 16). His response to this incredibly sad situation stands as an example and an encouragement to us. First, he writes, "May it not be charged against them!" (v. 16). Contrary to what we might expect, Paul covers the sins of his negligent friends with love. By the help of the Spirit, can we do the same for people who fail us? Second, Paul testifies to the hope of lonely Christians everywhere: "But the Lord stood by me and strengthened me" (v. 17). When you are alone, when you are longing for friends and finding none, the Lord is near. The One who was a friend to Abraham (see James 2:23) and to Paul will be your friend, too.

In your time as an elder's wife, you will doubtless experience times of loneliness. You can take encouragement from the example of Paul that a desire for friends is a good desire. What's more, as Paul did, you can humbly ask God to give you good friends while trusting him to be your dearest friend.

REFLECT. What aspects of being an elder's wife make it difficult for you to form and sustain friendships? Are any of these obstacles things that you can intentionally work around? What opportunities do you have as an elder's wife to befriend people whom you wouldn't otherwise know?

PRAY. Thank the Lord for good friends he has given you at various times in your life. Ask him to show you people in your church and community whom you could befriend. Ask him to draw near to you and comfort you in your loneliness.

ACT. Identify a woman who is in ministry and likely has little opportunity for friendship—perhaps someone who is on the foreign mission field or is laboring alongside her husband in a new church plant. Reach out to that woman in friendship. Ask her how you can pray for her, and commit to checking in with her periodically.

47. When Your Neighbors Reject You

These all died in faith, not having received the things
promised, but having seen them and greeted them
from afar, and having acknowledged that they were
strangers and exiles on the earth. (Heb. 11:13)

"Oh, man, you're a preacher's wife? I'd better watch myself."
I can't count the number of times I've heard some version of
these words. Hairstylists, plumbers, neighbors, coworkers, and
fellow soccer moms have all abruptly changed their casual attitude as soon as they discover my identity. My conversation with
them becomes awkward as they regret their earlier use of profan-
ity or the story that they blithely told about a drunken weekend.
I quickly affirm that I still want to talk to them, to know them,
to befriend them—but sometimes it's no use. To them, I'm just
different.

All Christians, says Peter, are "sojourners and exiles" whose
lives will be markedly different from the world around them (see
1 Peter 2:11). Believers' homes, schedules, finances, priorities,
and responsibilities don't look the same as those of our neighbors. Elders' wives may experience this alien status even more
pointedly. Because our husbands hold office in the church, we
can seem especially strange to unbelievers. They assume that
we must be more extreme than "ordinary" churchgoers are, and
they can feel more easily offended because of our official associa-
tion with the church. Our very presence in the room seems like a
black cloud of judgment.

Today's verse offers us two encouragements. First, it reminds
us that when we feel alienated from our neighbors, we are in good
company. Hebrews 11 contains a long list of saints who were
considered weird by the people around them. They sacrificed,
preached, relocated, and raised children for reasons that were

inscrutable to their pagan neighbors. And when your own convictions about the Lord's Day, the centrality of church worship, or the exclusive claims of Christ mean you are not welcome at the office watercooler, you can remember that this is how people treated "the prophets who were before you" (Matt. 5:12). When you feel most alone, you are not.

But not only does being strangers on this earth mean that we are in the company of all the saints, it also means that we are in Christ's company. When faced with the opportunity of fitting in to his surrounding pagan culture, Moses "considered the reproach of Christ greater wealth than the treasures of Egypt" (Heb. 11:26). Nonconformity to the world brings us into conformity with Christ. We know him, and the sufferings he experienced on our behalf, as we seek to live for his glory no matter what it costs us.

Hebrews 11 also encourages us that, one day, we won't be strangers anymore. What the saints saw "from afar" will come to pass. In eternity, we will join "a great multitude that no one [can] number, from every nation, from all tribes and peoples and languages, standing before the throne and before the Lamb" (Rev. 7:9). There, we will not be objects of curiosity or offense. We will not be shunned or scorned. We who belong to Christ will be eternally welcome.

REFLECT. In what situations do you feel most like an exile because you are a Christian? How does being an elder's wife exacerbate those feelings?

PRAY. Ask the Lord to give you the spirit of Moses—to cause you to clearly see the way of righteousness, to boldly choose Christ over sin, and to look forward to the eternal reward.

ACT. In the moment, it can be hard to know how to respond wisely when people say, "You're married to a church elder? Yikes!" Write out some possible scripts for what you can say in those situations.

48. When Your Extended Family Is Unsupportive

[Jesus replied], "Who is my mother, and who are my brothers?"
And stretching out his hand toward his disciples, he said, "Here are
my mother and my brothers! For whoever does the will of my Father
in heaven is my brother and sister and mother." (Matt. 12:48–50)

In a house in Galilee, Jesus was preaching. He was in the midst of a busy season of ministry—was traveling "through cities and villages, proclaiming and bringing the good news of the kingdom of God" (Luke 8:1). Everywhere he went, crowds gathered to hear his teaching and to seek healing (see Matt. 12:15). His disciples—the Twelve, along with a group of believing women—also followed him closely (see Luke 8:1–3). On this particular day, Jesus was "still speaking to the people" when a man interrupted him with a message (Matt. 12:46). Jesus's mother and brothers were outside, and they didn't seem to care that he was in the middle of his sermon; they wanted to talk to Jesus. *Now.*

Many elders' wives have experienced similar conflicts between ministry and family. Your siblings don't understand why you can't make their Sunday brunch. Your in-laws are angry that you are taking "their grandchildren" to a developing country in order to proclaim the good news of Christ. Your aunt is sweet, but she constantly hints that you are doing too much for your congregation and should really consider taking a break in order to practice more self-care. Your adult children joke sarcastically among themselves that it's no use calling Mom—ever!—because she's probably at church. Our family members often don't care about the responsibilities we have to Christ and his church; they want our time and attention, and they want it *now*.

In today's verses, Jesus helps us to navigate this family tension through his example and with his encouragement. First, he sets us an example. His family members, like many of ours, didn't want to be part of the congregation. They could have come in, but they "stood outside" (Matt. 12:46) and demanded that Jesus come to them—that he leave his obligations to the flock and prioritize their needs on their terms. Jesus refused (see v. 48). Sometimes we must prefer the cause of Christ and his church over our own family members. Jesus certainly taught the fifth commandment and lived it out through his own tender care for his mother (see Matt. 15:3–6; John 19:25–27). But his example in this passage teaches us that we do not answer to our families for the way we order our lives. We answer to the Lord.

This fact will probably cause relational difficulties. And here Jesus offers us encouragement. He may separate us from our biological families at times, but he brings us permanently into his own family. He declares us to be his mother and his brothers (see v. 49). Though our family members may be angry or embarrassed about our allegiance to Christ, he never distances himself from us. As the writer to the Hebrews affirms, "He is not ashamed to call them brothers" (2:11).

REFLECT. When have you felt unsupported by your extended family members? Why are relationships with unsupportive people particularly hard to navigate?

PRAY. Read Psalm 27:10: "For my father and my mother have forsaken me, but the Lord will take me in." Lament to the Lord the ways that your family has forsaken you because of him. Ask him to comfort you. Thank him for taking you in.

ACT. This week, when family members distance themselves or make demands that conflict with your commitment to Christ, remind yourself that Jesus understands your situation, loves you, and calls you his family.

49. When You Feel Far from Home

*By faith Abraham obeyed when he was called to
go out to a place that he was to receive as an inheritance.
And he went out, not knowing where he was going. . . .
For he was looking forward to the city that has foundations,
whose designer and builder is God. (Heb. 11:8, 10)*

In 1940, after years of language tutoring, months of separation from her young husband, and days of difficult jungle travel, Darlene Deibler Rose arrived at the remote Papua New Guinea village to which she and her husband hoped to bring the gospel of Jesus Christ. Darlene had left her dearest friends and most of her personal belongings behind in order to come to this village as the first non-native woman the villagers had ever seen. In her autobiography, she describes her moment of arrival: "Cresting the summit, I looked down into the valley and saw men, women, and children running out of their gardens or hurrying out of their huts. . . . My cheeks streaked with tears, I started running down the mountainside, singing at the top of my lungs, 'I'm home! I'm home!'"

Elders' wives are sometimes called to move. Whether that involves moving to a new neighborhood in order to better serve the church or moving to the other side of the world in order to plant a new church, we don't always get to live in the places that are comfortable or familiar to us. Like Darlene Deibler Rose, we leave behind the things and people we love: that favorite grocery store, those familiar woods, the friends from childhood. In other cases, elders' wives are called to stay—to assemble a second set of bunk beds in a too-small apartment because its location is ideal for gospel ministry.

Abraham also knew the discomfort of following God. Today's verses tell us that he "went out, not knowing where he was going." And his example can encourage us in our own struggles with living in the places where God has called us. First, Abraham had faith. He trusted that the God who had cared for him over the previous seventy-five years of his life would continue to care for him with every dusty step. This trust, then, enabled him to go where God called: "By faith Abraham obeyed." Our location, like our very lives, is Christ's to direct. And Abraham didn't obey with a sense of foreboding or grudging. He obeyed with joyful hope. He trusted the Lord's goodness to him in the near future (the new land was the "inheritance" God had promised his family), and he trusted the Lord's goodness to him in eternity (he fixed his eyes on "the city that has foundations"). Wherever we live and whatever we have had to give up, we too have Christ's promise that we will gain "a hundredfold" in this life and "in the age to come eternal life" (Mark 10:30).

REFLECT. Have you had to go to (or stay in) an uncomfortable place for the sake of the kingdom? In what ways was this hard? In what ways was it good?

PRAY. Confess the ways that you have failed to trust the Lord with your location, and ask him to give you hope as you obey his calling. Using the words of Psalm 90, ask him to remind you that *he* is your true and lasting home.

ACT. Make a list of things that bring you joy about your current location: a glimpse of the mountains, a place to read, neighborhood friends for your children, opportunities for the gospel. Remind yourself that God *is* blessing you where you are now—and set your eyes on your heavenly home.

CONCLUSION

50. I Am with You Always

"Go therefore and make disciples of all nations,
baptizing them in the name of the Father and of the
Son and of the Holy Spirit, teaching them to observe all
that I have commanded you. And behold, I am with you
always, to the end of the age." (Matt. 28:19–20)

Occasionally, an elder's wife in one of our previous churches would host the other elders' wives on an evening when our husbands had a meeting together. It was always a relief to leave behind my own dark, empty house and walk through the door of hers. She was an accomplished cook, and her kitchen would be filled with delicious aromas and the happy sound of women talking. We would eat dinner together and then enjoy one another's company. In the winter, we'd gather around a fire in her fireplace. In warmer months, we'd take cool glasses of iced tea out into her garden. On what would otherwise have been a long night, it was nice not to be alone.

Being an elder's wife can be lonely. In the previous pages, we've discussed dozens of ways in which ministry life presents particular joys and unique challenges. When we are members of elders' families, it can sometimes seem like no one else can quite understand our situation. Today we'll conclude with the words Jesus spoke before his ascension. In these instructions to his disciples—and, by extension, to his church—we'll see the comforting truth that Christ knows and cares for his people and promises to be with them.

The Great Commission is so well known that it can be easy to forget Jesus first spoke these words to a small group of his dearest friends. This foundational mission of the church was given to people whom Jesus knew intimately. He ate with them and traveled with them, he knew their personalities and their frailties, he prayed for them, and he died for them. So, too, your calling to kingdom faithfulness comes from the Savior who knows you completely. He knows your name and your weaknesses, he invites you to eat at his table, he prays for you, and he died for you. Christ knows you, and he also knows what he is asking of you. Making disciples is a task that requires the church to sacrifice and to suffer. We who are part of an elder's family often experience this acutely—but our Savior understands. If he calls you to face trials, they are trials that he willingly endured first. And he promises that you will not be alone. Although he ascended into the heavenly places, he leaves you with his Spirit, his Word, and his people. Through them, he instructs you, encourages you, warns you, guides you, and comforts you. Every moment of every day, Christ is near.

Dear sister, being an elder's wife is a unique calling—but remember this: Jesus will lead you by the hand, and he will never let you go.

REFLECT. When have you felt alone as an elder's wife? When have you experienced the Lord's care for you?

PRAY. Thank the Lord for calling you to be an elder's wife. Confess the times when you haven't trusted his care for you. Ask him to minister to you through his Spirit, his Word, and his people.

ACT. When you feel lonely today, meditate on your Savior. Remember that he knows you intimately and has cared for you every day of your life. Remember that he designed your calling as an elder's wife for your good and his glory. Remember that he promises you will never be alone.

ACKNOWLEDGMENTS

If I have anything to say to elders' wives, it is only because the elders' wives in my own life have taught me so much. From my childhood, I have belonged to five local churches, and the elders' wives in each one have loved me, prayed for me, served me, and set me an example of Christlikeness.

Of course, my own mother, Patsy Evans, will always be the original elder's wife to me. Her love for other people—welcoming them, caring for them, and demonstrating interest in them—is a virtue I'm still striving to match. Perhaps most importantly, she taught me by exhortation and example that ministry life is a good life. I owe much of my optimism about serving the church to her.

Along with my mom, a long line of faithful elders' wives have each shown me what it means to serve Christ and his beloved church. Freida Persons taught me all the kids' Scripture songs I know and shaped my childhood summers with her much-anticipated vacation Bible school (a.k.a. Fun Week). Ann Hughes and Anne Neikirk practiced seemingly tireless hospitality for our band of hungry college students. Cheryl Muscarella included me on her thrift store forays, played with my children, and repeatedly gave me a place to sit and rest. Gency Dykes faithfully encouraged me as a new (and not-so-new) pastor's wife. The elders' wives in my church today, to whom this book is dedicated, use their gifts to selflessly help their husbands for the good of our church. I hope to imitate them as they imitate Christ.

In addition to these women, and to so many others whose quiet prayer and sacrifice will be revealed in eternity, there are several elders' wives who belong to other churches but whose companionship refreshes my heart as well. Anne Severson, Michelle Gilbert, Cristy Slawson, Lindsey Carlson, Melissa Kruger, and Betsy Howard have each taught me about the privilege of caring for God's people. I'm grateful to call them my friends.

While writing this book, I had help from even more elders' wives: Kathy Ernst, Kathy Lee, Courtney Reissig, and my mom read my drafts and offered me practical perspectives and theological sharpening. No two elders' wives are exactly alike, and their unique personal experiences helped me to see beyond my own situation. The faults of this book are my own, but these women have a large share in its strengths.

And, as always, I'm thankful for my husband, Rob, who made me an elder's wife. He brought wisdom and clarity to these pages—as he does to my life. Serving the church alongside him is something I hope to do for a very, very long time.

NOTES

12 "The greatest need of my people": The source of this quote is uncertain, but M'Cheyne certainly affirmed its sentiment. See, for example, the letter he wrote to the Rev. E. C. Burns on March 22, 1839, which appears in Andrew A. Bonar, *Memoir and Remains of the Rev. Robert Murray M'Cheyne, Minister of St Peter's Church, Dundee*, 2nd ed. (Dundee, Scotland, 1845), 178–79.

22 to glorify and enjoy God: See the Westminster Shorter Catechism, answer 1.

30 paragraph about Jim: I have also told Jim's story in *A Place to Belong: Learning to Love the Local Church* (Wheaton, IL: Crossway, 2020), 17–18.

36 "People who know their God": J. I. Packer, *Knowing God*, 20th anniv. ed. (Downers Grove, IL: IVP Books, 1993), 28.

38 "withdraws His normal operation": Wilhelmus à Brakel, "Spiritual Desertion," in *The Christian's Reasonable Service*, trans. Bartel Elshout, ed. Joel R. Beeke (repr., Grand Rapids: Reformation Heritage Books, 1992) 4:174.

38 the next three sentences after the above quote: See à Brakel, 4:180–82.

38 "the empty hand of the soul": Thomas Manton, *James*, Geneva

Series of Commentaries (1693; repr., Carlisle, PA: Banner of Truth, 1998), 455.

42 paragraph about Margaret Baxter: See Sharon James, "Margaret Baxter," in *In Trouble and in Joy: Four Women Who Lived for God* (Auburn, MA: Evangelical Press, 2003), 21–66.

58 "Do you now unreservedly dedicate": *The Book of Church Order of the Presbyterian Church in America* (Lawrenceville, GA: The Office of the Stated Clerk of the General Assembly of the Presbyterian Church of America, 2019), 56–5.

60 "There is no specific kind of house": Edith Schaeffer, *The Hidden Art of Homemaking: Creative Ideas for Enriching Everyday Life* (1971; repr., Wheaton, IL: Tyndale, 1985), 110.

69 "There is a safety and assurance": Gloria Furman, *The Pastor's Wife: Strengthened by Grace for a Life of Love* (Wheaton, IL: Crossway, 2015), 36–37.

70 "Marriage is not a thing of nature": Martin Luther, *Table Talk*, vol. 4 (Eisleben, Germany, 1566), no. 4786, quoted in Jeff Robinson, "The Luther Family and the Reformation of Marriage," The Gospel Coalition, October 25, 2017, https://www.thegospelcoalition.org/reviews/katharina-and-martin-luther-radical-marriage/.

76 "No matter the magnitude": Janie Street, "Habitual Sin in the Life of My Husband: Now What?" in *Letters to Pastors' Wives: When Seminary Ends and Ministry Begins*, ed. Catherine J. Stewart (Phillipsburg, NJ: P&R Publishing, 2013), 249.

99 "I am not my own but belong": "The Heidelberg Catechism (1563)" in *Reformed Confessions of the 16th and 17th Centuries in English Translation*, comp. James T. Dennison Jr., vol. 2, *1552–1566* (Grand Rapids: Reformation Heritage Books, 2010), answer 1.

100 "Wifey . . . don't you see": *C. H. Spurgeon's Autobiography: Compiled from His Diary, Letters, and Records, by His Wife, and His Private Secretary*, vol. 2, *1854–1860* (London, 1898), 187.

102 "So many times you have disappointed me": Gloria Furman, *The Pastor's Wife: Strengthened by Grace for a Life of Love* (Wheaton, IL: Crossway, 2015), 49.

102 "The most unspotted innocency": *Matthew Henry's Commentary on the Whole Bible*, vol. 5, *Matthew to John* (1710; repr., Peabody, MA: Hendrickson, 1991), 126.

103 "And now I'm beginning to realize": Gloria Furman, *The Pastor's Wife: Strengthened by Grace for a Life of Love* (Wheaton, IL: Crossway, 2015), 49.

118 this church partnered with his gospel work in three important ways: See William Hendriksen, *Exposition of Philippians*, New Testament Commentary (1962; repr., Grand Rapids: Baker Book House, 1979), 52.

122 paragraph about Sara: Sara's family graciously gave me permission to tell her story here.

137 "Cresting the summit, I looked down": Darlene Deibler Rose, *Evidence Not Seen: A Woman's Miraculous Faith in the Jungles of World War II* (1988; repr., San Francisco: HarperOne, 2003), 28.

BIBLIOGRAPHY

à Brakel, Wilhelmus. "Spiritual Desertion." In *The Christian's Reasonable Service*. Translated by Bartel Elshout. Edited by Joel R. Beeke. Vol. 4, 171–91. Reprint, Grand Rapids: Reformation Heritage Books, 1992.

Bonar, Andrew A. *Memoir and Remains of the Rev. Robert Murray M'Cheyne, Minister of St Peter's Church, Dundee*. 2nd ed. Dundee, Scotland, 1845.

The Book of Church Order of the Presbyterian Church in America. Lawrenceville, GA: The Office of the Stated Clerk of the General Assembly of the Presbyterian Church in America, 2019.

Dennison, James T., Jr., comp. *Reformed Confessions of the 16th and 17th Centuries in English Translation*. Vol. 2, *1552–1566*. Grand Rapids: Reformation Heritage Books, 2010.

Furman, Gloria. *The Pastor's Wife: Strengthened by Grace for a Life of Love*. Wheaton, IL: Crossway, 2015.

Hendriksen, William. *Exposition of Philippians*. New Testament Commentary. 1962. Reprint, Grand Rapids: Baker Book House, 1979.

Henry, Matthew. *Matthew Henry's Commentary on the Whole Bible*. Vol. 5, *Matthew to John*. 1710. Reprint, Peabody, MA: Hendrickson, 1991.

Hill, Megan. *A Place to Belong: Learning to Love the Local Church.* Wheaton, IL: Crossway, 2020.

James, Sharon. *In Trouble and in Joy: Four Women Who Lived for God.* Auburn, MA: Evangelical Press, 2003.

Manton, Thomas. *James.* Geneva Series of Commentaries. 1693. Reprint, Carlisle, PA: Banner of Truth, 1998.

Packer, J. I. *Knowing God.* Twentieth anniversary ed. Downers Grove, IL: IVP Books, 1993.

Robinson, Jeff. "The Luther Family and the Reformation of Marriage." The Gospel Coalition. October 25, 2017. https://www.tgc.org /reviews/katharina-and-martin-luther-radical-marriage/.

Rose, Darlene Deibler. *Evidence Not Seen: A Woman's Miraculous Faith in the Jungles of World War II.* 1988. Reprint, San Francisco: HarperOne, 2003.

Schaeffer, Edith. *The Hidden Art of Homemaking: Creative Ideas for Enriching Everyday Life.* 1971. Reprint, Wheaton, IL: Tyndale, 1985.

Spurgeon, C. H. *C. H. Spurgeon's Autobiography: Compiled from His Diary, Letters, and Records, by His Wife, and His Private Secretary.* Vol. 2, *1854–1860.* London, 1898.

Stewart, Catherine J., ed. *Letters to Pastors' Wives: When Seminary Ends and Ministry Begins.* Phillipsburg, NJ: P&R Publishing, 2013.

The Westminster Confession of Faith Together with the Larger Catechism and the Shorter Catechism with Scripture Proofs. 3rd ed. Lawrenceville, GA: Christian Education & Publications, 1990.